NIMBLE

Cincinnati, Ohio
www.howdesign.com

NIMBLE

Thinking Creatively in the Digital Age

ROBIN LANDA

For more excellent books and resources for designers, visit
www.howdesign.com.

19 18 17 16 15   5 4 3 2 1

ISBN-13: 978-1-4403-3757-4

Distributed in Canada by Fraser Direct
100 Armstrong Avenue
Georgetown, Ontario, Canada L7G 5S4
Tel: (905) 877-4411

Distributed in the U.K. and Europe by F&W Media International, LTD
Brunel House, Forde Close, Newton Abbot, TQ12 4PU, UK
Tel: (+44) 1626 323200, Fax: (+44) 1626 323319
Email: enquiries@fwmedia.com

Distributed in Australia by Capricorn Link
P.O. Box 704, Windsor, NSW 2756 Australia
Tel: (02) 4560-1600

Edited by Scott Francis and Amy Owen
Cover designed by Max Friedman
Interior designed by Claudean Wheeler
Production coordinated by Greg Nock

a content + ecommerce company

Dedication
For Hayley, my favorite nimble thinker.

Acknowledgments

I humbly thank and am indebted to Denise Anderson, Mark Avnet, Liz Blazer, Paula Bosco, Stefan G. Bucher, Kill Cooper, Kaila Edmondson, Dave Glass, Dr. Peter Gray, Scott Francis, Max Friedman, Rei Inamoto, Dr. Mizuko Ito, Sarah Nelson Jackson, Jean-Marc Joseph, Matt Lyon, Denyse Mitterhofer, Mariko Oda, Amy Owen, Josh Owen, Payam, PJ Pereira, Tish Scolnik, Jennifer Sterling, Ashley Stewart, Brian Storm, Patrick Sutherland, Dr. Jeffrey H. Toney, Ria R. Venturina, Steve Vranakis, Jessica Walsh, John Weigele, and Claudean Wheeler for their excellent and generous contributions to this book.

At Kean University, I would like to express my gratitude to Dr. Dawood Farahi, President; Dr. Jeffrey H. Toney, Provost and Vice President of Academic Affairs; Prof. Rose Gonnella, Executive Director of the Robert Busch School of Design; Dr. Susan Gannon, Office for Research and Sponsored Programs; the Release Time for Research committee for the research grant; and all of my other esteemed colleagues.

I would also like to thank my dear Robert Busch School of Design students, who deserve nothing less than nimble pedagogy. I hope I have inspired and provided the tools for lifelong learning.

And finally—loving thanks to my husband Dr. Harry Gruenspan and our darling daughter Hayley.

CONTENTS

CHAPTER 06.

INTERVIEWS

EMBRACING THE NEW CHALLENGES

> *"Complacency is the number one killer of creativity. Keep moving."*
> —**STEVE VRANAKIS**, Executive Creative Director, Creative Lab, Google

How does one flourish in design today? How does one avoid becoming a person who is out of place, an anachronistic thinker, a fogy—or perhaps worse, someone with limited scope or capabilities?

Technology is progressing rapidly. That's not a qualitative statement—it's a fact. Very soon cars that drive themselves will transport us and most of us will be sporting wearable computers. All the rapid technological changes have altered the nature of work, people's habits and consequently what designers need to be able to do. In the ages past, life was short and art was long. Today, life is long and tech is short.

Employers want to hire nimble thinkers: people who are not only content experts but who also are agile in adapting to new technology and new directions in their fields. With rapid technological changes and globalization, the ability to think creatively and strategically is crucial.

These nimble thinkers not only keep up, but they also better serve people by sharpening their thinking. Steve Vranakis, Executive Creative Director, Creative Lab, Google, believes that "technology combined with creativity can be used as a force for good and allow for people to come up with ideas that change the world."

> *"[N]ow, even more than in the past, creativity is a key to economic success. We no longer need people to follow directions in robot-like ways (we have robots for that), or to perform routine calculations (we have computers for that), or to answer already-answered questions (we have search engines for that). But we do need people who can ask and seek answers to new questions, solve new problems and anticipate obstacles before they arise. These all require the ability to think creatively. The creative mind is a playful mind."*
> —**PETER GRAY, PH.D.**, Research Professor, Boston College

Embracing Change

If you're a nimble thinker you can change with the times. If you're an imaginative thinker, you might be able to disrupt current paradigms or engage in world building (think of the worlds built by J.K. Rowling's fiction, Wes Anderson's films, or think of J. Mayer H. Architects' Metropol Parasol or the Creative Artists Agency Chipotle short films).

If you can fundamentally change a business model, product or service, you can shift the paradigm. For example, packages are supposed to be delivered by the carrier's workforce. As you'll learn in chapter 1, DHL created MyWays to facilitate last-mile deliveries throughout Stockholm by crowdsourcing to the city's residents. This new model disrupts the ordinary business model of delivery services.

There's more than one way to deliver a package, it seems—and nimble thinkers know there are many ways to do many things. For Austin's South by Southwest (SXSW) festival, GSD&M, an Austin-based ad agency, developed an app called Avoid Humans, which uses Foursquare data and a curated list of high quality bars, cafes and restaurants to help users find the *least* crowded places in town.

So is the new creativity a disruptive model? Being forward thinking—what Bloomberg TV calls a game changer—certainly takes imagination, ingenuity and knowledge. Think of Steve Jobs, Sergey Brin and Larry Page,

Martin Cooper and Mark Zuckerberg. Think of creative solutions such as R/GA's Nike+ platform, Crispin Porter + Bogusky's "Subservient Chicken" for Burger King, Otto Neurath's Isotype (the International System of Typographic Picture Education), Saul Bass's film title sequences, Alex Steinweiss's album covers, Jonathan Ive's work for Apple or Google Glass, and Jake Dyson's LED light that lasts 50 years—or other companies and entities who innovate such as Netflix, Dropbox, MakerBot, SXSW, Twitter and Bloomberg Philanthropies.

There are many ways to innovate or think creatively. One must assess each situation with a creative and judicious mind-set. Patrick Sutherland, Founder of Vidoovy, offers practical advice, "In the end applying any approach to a new situation just because it worked the last time is a recipe for failure. This includes disruption. Instead survey the terrain as it changes and make your best judgment based on probabilities that exist at that moment."

AN ASSESSMENT GUIDE

Use these topics and questions as you evaluate your work. I'll also refer to them throughout the book.

CLARITY: Will your idea communicate clearly and quickly?

POSSIBLE: Can your idea be implemented?

CREATIVITY: Is your concept inspiring or unique?

FORWARD THINKING: Is your concept a game changer? Does it disrupt the current model?

CRAFT: Does the execution best serve the concept? Is it well crafted?

MEDIA CHANNEL: Are you taking advantage of what the media channel can do? Can you do anything exciting with the channel that hasn't been done before?

SOCIAL PROPOSITION: Does it benefit people or society? (Imbuing a brand or product design with a social proposition—with an inherent or deliberated benefit to society is logical and requires creative thinking to generate and implement; it serves all involved.)

Thinking Without a Playbook

What if you did not have a playbook? No conventions or rules? What if you were the first designer to ever design what you're about to do? Thinking without a playbook frees us from conventional thinking. Every semester, I have to combat my students' tendency to make their solutions look like what they think a design or advertising solution is supposed to look like—like pedestrian solutions they've seen a million times.

Dave Glass (aka Danger) of Hungry Castle, remarks, "There is no guaranteed creative process. Sometimes we start with a problem that needs to be solved. Other times we start with a solution that actually requires a problem. That might sound like some artsy-fartsy crap right there but it's true." (See the full interview with Hungry Castle's Dave Glass and Kill Cooper in chapter 6.)

When I asked PJ Pereira, Chief Creative Officer and Cofounder of Pereira & O'Dell, about the agency's guiding principle, he replied, "We ask ourselves, 'What if advertising had no history? What if advertising were invented today, the day we got the assignment?' That approach frees our thinking; it frees us to use our tools to defy conventional categories." (See the full interview with PJ Pereira in chapter 6.)

Embrace change. In contemporary times, change is continuous. Prepare for it by learning more and broadly and by sharpening your cognitive domain skills, the core learning domain involving the development of critical thinking: knowledge, comprehension, analysis, synthesis and evaluation.

Embracing daily the goals of being nimble and thinking creatively will trigger the release of endorphins in your brain—and that will feel good.

How This Content Will Help You Be Nimble

Employers want creatives who can generate big ideas: platforms that build community, branded utilities, content as branded entertainment that is so good it competes with all entertainment, disruptive ideas that benefit everyone (client, individuals and society), marketing as service, products that make lives better, and value creation in everything.

Here's what you'll take away from this book:

- imagination preparation so that original works and ideas can emerge
- critical and creative thinking tools
- understanding of how to create content people will find engaging, relevant or beneficial
- the ability to problem find: to anticipate or foresee a problem and solution rather than only solving assigned problems
- enhanced creativity through executing the book's exercises
- insights from the interviews with esteemed experts
- the habit of creative and critical thinking and observing

CHAPTER 01

THINKING CREATIVELY

> *"In today's rapidly changing world, people must continually come up with creative solutions to unexpected problems. Success is based not only on what you know or how much you know, but on your ability to think and act creatively. In short, we are now living in the Creative Society."* —**MITCHEL RESNICK**, LEGO Papert Professor of Learning Research Academic Head, Program in Media Arts and Sciences, MIT Media Lab

THE CHALLENGE

Generating viable ideas and creating in the digital age presents new challenges for all designers. Employers and clients call upon creative professionals to quickly conceive and execute grand ideas and react nimbly to rapid changes in industries, technology and business sectors. Graphic designers need to be empathetic, interdisciplinary story-makers working across media. They must fully understand what each specific media channel can do and how each channel can be utilized to deliver an engaging brand experience, contributing an integral element of the brand narrative. It's essential that designers generate concepts for a campaign or program that take various forms related by strategy, voice and design across channels, ranging from print to social films to websites to mobile apps to web platforms.

> *"Our goal is to design everything so it's beautifully simple."*
> —**LARRY PAGE**, Cofounder, Google

Many graphic designers, art directors, copywriters, and creative directors face the new challenge of creating **relevant** *original content* for brands, causes and organizations to market online and in social media. Part of this challenge entails understanding how people behave online, become cocreators, and use technology, mobile and social media. Unique content must give people a story to tell, one that engages them enough to talk about or share online.

Industrial designers need to address unexpected challenges to meet market needs. They address usability issues and generate design concepts that address social issues facing the global community. Reconsidering what functional objects are all about—whether reinventing the concept of a car or a soccer ball, or wheelchair or eyeglasses—requires keen imaginations that synthesize need, beauty, function and experience.

To face these new challenges, consider:

1. Viewing a design or visual communication problem with a new mind-set.
2. Cultivating your creative thinking and preparing your imagination.
3. Becoming a design expert with additional knowledge gained by keen interest in a broad range of subjects.

A New Mind-Set

Let's begin to adapt our thinking about design, branding or advertising solutions by thinking of it as content creation rather than as creating an artifact.

Rather than thinking about solving a problem, approach the visual communication goals with an open, experimental mind-set. To do this, set aside the closed conventions of what design or advertising is supposed to be. Instead strive to understand how to make a brand social and create content and product design that people will find engaging, relevant or beneficial. Ask: Is the idea flexible? Is it entertaining? Is it informative? Does it have value? Will it positively impact society? Does the idea inspire content that people will share? How will the idea manifest and function for the capabilities of specific channels and platforms?

The motto of this new mindset is: Entertain. Inform. Be useful. Do good.

Imagination Prep

In the design professions (graphic design, industrial design, product design, advertising design and interior architecture design), a problem is given and you have to solve it. However, to solve a given problem well, a designer must learn to think like a scientist rather than a detective. My premise goes back to Albert Einstein and Leopold Infeld in 1938:

> For the detective the crime is given, the problem formulated: Who killed Cock Robin? The scientist must, at least in part, commit his own crime as well as carry out the investigation. ... The formulation of a problem is often more essential than its solution, which may be merely a matter of mathematical or experimental skill. To raise new questions, new possibilities, to regard old questions from a new angle, requires creative imagination and marks real advance in science.

This holds true in design too. Your goal is to prepare your imagination so that original works and ideas can emerge. This is a developed capacity. We have to enhance our imaginations like fine artists: for instance, René Magritte took the familiar and made it strange and Odilon Redon took the strange and made it familiar.

T-Shaped Connector

A T-shaped creative is a content expert with additional knowledge in a broad range of subjects she's interested in that gives her thinking depth and breadth. The vertical bar of the *T* represents expertise and skills in one's field of study and practice; the horizontal bar of the *T* represents knowledge in areas other than one's own, interest in other disciplines, and subject matter and the capacity to collaborate across fields with other experts. David Guest first employed the term (in an editorial in the London newspaper, *The Independent*, in 1991); designer Bill Moggridge of IDEO made the term popular. Moggridge explains that design creates a bridge between the sciences and the arts. So if designers are to create that bridge, they must think richly and broadly—they must be T-shaped thinkers.

Let's take this T-shaped thinking further: depth and breadth are enhanced by making connections amidst one's broad knowledge base, as well as actively seeking connections. It helps to be a meta-thinker (an awareness of or an analysis of one's own thinking) in order to better understand how one is processing material.

It's imperative to stay abreast of the latest in technology (in all design disciplines, not only your own), disruptive business models, art, and research in the social sciences (sociology, economics, anthropology and psychology) that directly impact design. Use what you learn to conceive, construct or figure out. Experiment.

Share your knowledge with colleagues and find out what they're learning. As a resource, start a diverse creative community for cross-pollination. Spread the gospel of the T-thinking mind-set to help designers expand their knowledge base moving beyond their own area of expertise. Innovation often happens at the intersection of two disciplines. To innovate in that way, you need knowledge of more than one field.

DELIVERABLES

The question on most every consumer's mind is *What's in it for me?* Whether by entertaining or providing a utility as a benefit, many brands are answering that concern instead of deploying the faded one-way marketing message of a television commercial or print ad.

This isn't an entirely new concept, but it is more important than ever. In 1900, Michelin brand published their first *Michelin Red Guide*. The guide's website (www.michelintravel.com/about) explains, "André and Edouard Michelin foresaw that for the automobile to be successful, motorists had to be able to find places to refuel, charge their batteries or change their tires wherever they traveled. The MICHELIN guide was therefore created to offer drivers all of this useful information, free of charge."

Digital channels allow marketers to pull in audiences with entertaining film, free apps, games or other content. BMW and agency Fallon helped usher in advertising content that was appealing enough to pull people in (as opposed to advertising that is pushed at people, such as TV commercials) in 2001 with a web film campaign called "The Hire" starring Clive Owen as the BMW's driver. The campaign featured films by esteemed movie directors, including John Frankenheimer, Ang Lee and Tony Scott and featured celebrities such as James Brown and Madonna in addition to Clive Owen. More examples of effective deliverables follow to give you an idea of the kind of nimble thinking necessary today to answer the consumer question, "What can you do for me?"

Social Film: The Beauty Inside

Even though he's the same person on the inside, every day Alex wakes up looking like a different person. When he meets Leah and falls in love with her, "He knows he will see her again but she will never see him." *The Beauty Inside* is Alex's story—a social film Pereira & O'Dell created for Intel and Toshiba. Imaginatively, this romance allows anyone, male or female, to play the film's lead role of Alex. "Through social channels, Intel and Toshiba invited the audience to play the lead role of Alex by auditioning online. Fans could also interact with Alex on Facebook in between episodes."

It was directed by Sundance winner Drake Doremus, stars Topher Grace, Mary Elizabeth Winstead and Matthew Gray Gubler, and won numerous prestigious awards (including Cannes Branded Content and Entertainment Grand Prix, Grand Clios, as well as a Daytime Emmy in the category of Outstanding New Approaches: Original Daytime Program or Series). "The Beauty Inside" exemplifies the kind of imaginative thinking it takes to create marketing that pulls people in and that's shareworthy.

Computer Application: eco:Drive

Agency AKQA told the story of Fiat cars' fuel-efficiency. To engage drivers, they created the Cannes Cyber Grand Prix winning eco:Drive, an easy to use computer application. Fiat wanted to find a way to "tell the story of the fuel-efficiency of Fiat cars in a way that was simple, human and fun" (www.mediapost.com/publications/article/158006/the-browser-akqa.html?print).

Users download the application from the Fiat website to a computer, then save it on any USB stick. Insert the USB stick into the Fiat port. Drive. Then plug the USB stick into the computer. The technology evaluates the driver's style and other data and recommends "how to reduce fuel consumption, and save money and the planet. Fiat sold one million eco:Drive enabled cars. The 30,000 residents of eco:Ville reduced CO2 emissions by 2.6 million kilograms—enough to cook them dinner for 144 days" (www.akqa.com/#/work/fiat/eco-drive/idea).

(See the interview with AKQA's Chief Creative Officer Rei Inamoto in chapter 6.)

Platform: Nike+

Employers want creatives who can generate grand ideas such as the one behind the Nike+ proprietary platform and design created by R/GA. This platform allows runners to track multiple activities, compare results over time, find better routes, train smarter, challenge friends, describe their day, improve their performances and post their success. The Nike+ platform builds community and the brand as well as providing services. (Learn more at http://nikeplus.nike.com/plus.)

Platform: That's Not Cool

Another example of the kind of creative solution is the That's Not Cool digital platform, also created by R/GA for Futures Without Violence, "to help teens get informed, cope with digital harassment, and draw their own digital line separating acceptable from inappropriate" (from www.thatsnotcool.com). To help teens draw their own digital line, the advertising design team created the That's Not Cool mobile site. "Teens are inseparable from their devices, so with the mobile site, they're never more than a click away from help. We developed call out cards with quirky yet firm messages that teens could send to peers, right from the mobile site, to let them know they're crossing the line. They could also learn about digital abuse, share experiences, and get professional help."

App: Feedie

The Feedie app from Omnicom benefits The Lunchbox Fund. "Feedie is an app... that transforms your passion for sharing food photos into actually sharing food for those who need it. Simply sign up via Facebook or Twitter, and visit a participating restaurant. When you use Feedie to take a photo of your meal and post it, the restaurant makes a donation to The Lunchbox Fund—a non-profit organization that provides daily meals to schoolchildren in South Africa. Your post thanks the restaurant and spreads the Feedie message!" The app's creators combined function, social impact and creating thinking in this solution. (Find out more at www.wethefeedies.com.)

Program: Red Bull Stratos

Red Bull's story is an action story, very fitting for this beverage category. As part of the The Red Bull Stratos mission, supported by an expert team, Austrian skydiver and BASE jumper Felix Baumgartner "ascended to 128,100 feet in a stratospheric balloon and made a freefall jump rushing toward earth at supersonic speeds before parachuting to the ground" (www.redbullstratos.com).

According to Red Bull, "The primary contribution to the science community includes data that could help develop next generation space suits, establish viable escape procedures for passengers and crew in space, and create parachutes with state-of-the-art safety systems." Red Bull also supports hundreds of athletes worldwide.

Campaign: Dumb Ways to Die

Highly likeable and shareable, "Dumb Ways to Die" ensured that young people paid attention to a message about safety from Metro Trains Melbourne, and it gave those young people something to talk about. "Dumb Ways to Die" (DWTD) became a global phenomenon; it was the most awarded campaign in the sixty-year history of the Cannes Lions International Festival of Creativity. According to Metro Trains, the campaign contributed to a more than 30 percent reduction in near-miss accidents.

McCann Melbourne, the ad agency, "understood that early adopters would be key to success," so they "amplified shareability by creating .gifs from the video animation and shared them via Tumblr" (www.interpublic.com/our-agencies/recent-works?work_id=2510&casename=Dumb+Ways+To+Die).

"After writing the first comment on the YouTube video, which provided the links to buy the song on iTunes or listen/download via Soundcloud, McCann Melbourne... did not engage in the online commentary in any way and have continued to be entirely non-interventional. This freedom has allowed people to create multiple translations that have facilitated growth throughout Asia, Europe and South America."

Mobile App: DHL MyWays

To facilitate last-mile deliveries throughout Stockholm, DHL introduced MyWays, an original business model that crowdsources to the city's residents. Deutsche Post DHL's Innovation unit developed the concept.

The app's website (www.myways.com) explains it this way: "Don't have time to pick up your parcel from the DHL Service Point? No problem! All you need to do is install the new MyWays App on your smartphone and add the parcel to the platform. To do so you need to insert the DHL Tracking number, select time and places where you want to receive the parcel and also choose how much you are willing to pay for the delivery."

Using the MyWays mobile app, DHL customers who request flexible deliveries connect with people (mostly students) offering to transport packages along their daily routes to earn a little extra income. All connections and details are worked out using the mobile app. This innovative model disrupts the ordinary business model of delivery services. In this case, the new creativity is a disruptive model.

CHAPTER 02

THE NEW CREATIVITY PREP SCHOOL

> *"Innovation is not the product of logical thought, although the result is tied to logical structure."* —ALBERT EINSTEIN

WORKING BACKWARDS THROUGH PROBLEM FINDING AND DECONSTRUCTION

To endow our work with artistry, rather than mimic what has been done before, we need to prepare our minds. Thinking imaginatively prevents the creation of pedestrian solutions. Scientist Louis Pasteur said, "Chance favors only the prepared mind." We need to add to our *preparatory practice* to free ourselves from conventions in order to be ready to design or create in a wired world. We need to be prepared to create content and design that promotes, informs, performs, serves, solves, entertains, or engages.

Johannes Itten understood the critical nature of preparing in a free way. In *Mein Vorkurs am Bauhaus: Gestaltung und Formenlehrehis,* Itten explains one of the goals of his Bauhaus Preparatory course: "To free the creative forces and thus the artistic talents of the students. Individual experience and insights were to lead to real work. The students were to free themselves step by step from all dead conventions and pluck up the courage to do their work."

Whether to serve commerce and brands or to serve human rights and the social good, new preparatory creative thinking is crucial and should be robust.

> *"Most conversations between a brand and its consumers begin with a piece of content."*
> —JONATHAN MILDENHALL, Chief Marketing Officer, Airbnb

PROBLEM-FINDING PROMPTS

Problem solving is the prevailing paradigm across design disciplines: Designers problem solve. In practice, though, this paradigm inhibits them from behaving like most fine artists who create until a discovery or a direction emerges. Only once a discovery emerges do fine artists use that journey to generate and crystalize a creative problem to solve. Henri-Georges Clouzot's 1956 documentary, *The Mystery of Picasso (Le Mystère Picasso)*, sets out to understand the "mystery" of Pablo Picasso's creative process. In this groundbreaking film, we see Picasso at work. As we watch Picasso paint, we realize his process is spontaneous: each form he paints brings him to another—nothing was preconceived. Five hours into the process, as his free form association continues, Picasso declares that he will have to discard the canvas: "Now that I begin to see where I'm going with it, I'll take a new canvas and start again." Picasso used the painting process to find inspiration and direction; he painted to seek an idea. Nothing was planned.

The following methodology uses a discovery-led paradigm that draws upon a fine art creative process coupled with a design directive (a technique, topic, a story starter, a prompt to incite action) resulting in a novel process for designers or any creative visual artist.

Because designers now create unique content for brands or organizations, these exercises aim to encourage T-thinking—broadening and deepening one's knowledge base—in order to generate unique content and ideas.

After you generate content or designs, you deconstruct what you've shaped to determine if it could be used to serve a branded product or service

PROJECT TIPS FOR THINKING CREATIVELY

- Use words or sketches to think. Go old school with a pencil or marker in your hand. Drawing engages most regions of your brain.

- Begin with research. Dr. Mizuko Ito advises: "Finding out about a new interest or seeking an answer to a thorny problem can be as simple as Googling, finding a YouTube video, or lurking on an expert forum. FAQs, tutorials, how-to videos and detailed answers on Q&A forums litter the Internet, created by experts, enthusiasts and hobbyists of all shapes and sizes." (See full interview with Dr. Ito in chapter 6.)

- Collaborate if you can. Find other discipline experts—perhaps you know a psychologist or IT expert. Or work with someone in the same discipline who complements your mindset or skill set—someone with whom you have collaborative chemistry. (Author Joshua Wolf Shenk builds an argument that one-to-one collaboration drives creative success in his book, *Powers of Two: Seeking the Essence of Innovation in Creative Pairs.* Think of John Lennon and Paul McCartney, Marie and Pierre Curie, or Steve Jobs and Steve Wozniak.)

- If you run into a creative roadblock, try free writing or free drawing. Or try mind mapping: Write a word or sketch an object in the center of a page. Extend lines out from that central word or sketch and write or draw whatever comes to mind next.

or a social cause or nonprofit organization, or if it could be used as a design tool or object. Analyze the subject matter, style and suitability. This analysis itself is highly instructive—deconstructing images to understand them, analyzing style for meaning, and finally determining if the original content is appropriate for a brand or organization, on-brand (in sync with the core brand narrative) or off-brand (not in sync with the core brand narrative).

When you learn something new, dopamine levels increase in the brain, which is why creative challenges make you feel good. So jump in and try any or all of the following exercises.

Devise and Design a Commitment Device

Yielding to immediate gratification is tempting. Many of us can relate to indulging ourselves even though we know our present actions may not be in the best interest of our future selves. In a TED talk, Daniel Goldstein, Principal Researcher at Microsoft, spoke about "The Battle Between Your Present and Future Self." Goldstein pointed out that many employ "commitment devices" to aid or enforce self-control, to make a firm agreement with ourselves to deter ourselves from poor judgment later.

Goldstein explains (from www.businessinsider.com/dan-goldstein-ted-talk-2013-5#ixzz2x6WrypOG): "It's an unequal battle between the present self and the future self. I mean, let's face it, the present self is present. It's in control. It's in power right now. It has these strong, heroic arms that can lift doughnuts into your mouth. And the future self is not even around. It's off in the future. It's weak. It doesn't even have a lawyer present. There's nobody to stick up for the future self. And so the present self can trounce all over its dreams. So how do we better resist temptation? By imagining ourselves more clearly in the future, as products of our decisions."

According to University of Chicago economist Steven D. Levitt and *New York Times* journalist Stephen J. Dubner, authors of *Freakonomics,* a commitment device is "a means to lock yourself into a course of action that you might not otherwise choose but that produces a desired result."

Let's say someone wants to ensure she keeps to her workout regimen. She could oblige herself to do a friend's laundry every time she skips a

---

"Experimentation, exploration, and social exchange have always been central to meaningful learning. Today's online world, which includes rich content as well as social media, offers an abundance of opportunity for exploratory and social learning."

—**MIZUKO ITO, PH.D.**, Cultural Anthropologist and Professor in Residence and John D. and Catherine T. MacArthur Foundation Chair in Digital Media and Learning, Department of Anthropology and Department of Informatics, University of California, Irvine

---

workout. An early example of such a device is in Homer's *The Odyssey*. When Odysseus and his crew were sailing home to Ithaca their ship would pass the coast of the Sirens—sea nymphs who have the power of charming those who hear their song. Odysseus wanted to hear their song but to avoid the consequences of being lured by the Sirens he directed his seamen to plug their ears with wax and tie him to the mast and not untie him no matter how he pleaded or tried to set himself free. This commitment device ensured that Odysseus' ship would stay the course home to Ithaca.

Your commitment device can take any form: digital, object, tool, ceremony, game app, activity, and more. Once you devise it, deconstruct it for relevance to a brand or cause—for what product, service or organization could you use this content? For instance, a commitment device about saving money could relate to a bank or college fund brand known to be family-oriented or, a bit less obviously, to a vacation resort. A diet plan in the form of a mobile game app could be related to the Let's Move! program (www.letsmove.gov), developed by Michelle Obama to solve the epidemic of childhood obesity within a generation.

Offer Ten Tips to a College Freshman
Here's the scenario: You've taken a college freshman under your wing. Decide the following stats about your freshman: gender, which college, hobbies and interests, mode of transportation, food and apparel preferences, cultural communities, and reading or viewing list.

Based on these details, present ten tips for navigating college life.

Once you have a working list, figure out which brand or group you could use this content for. A university could utilize your list as a promotion, or less obviously, a coffeehouse brand found on university campuses or a ramen noodles brand could use your content for a promotion. Determine how any branded product, service or organization could best utilize this unique content to interest or benefit people and how the content would be distributed to people (social media channels, apps, print [posters, coffee wraps, etc.], mobile notices, wearables, and more).

Here are two examples of lists.

1. Don't be a jerk.
2. Be active in class—try to talk to people.
3. If possible, don't procrastinate.
4. Register for classes as soon as possible.
5. Get to school early to find a parking spot.
6. Take the required general education classes early.
7. Find the right balance of classes for you.
8. Take classes you're actually interested in.
9. Don't buy the books unless you know you need them.
10. Don't make college your whole life.

Written by Caitlin Danko, Mike DeBisco, Sean McCluskey and Stefanie Osmond who are students at the Robert Busch School of Design, Kean University.

1. Manage your time well.
2. Have all your materials.
3. Be on time.
4. Get to know as many people as you can.
5. Get to know your professors.
6. Try to go to activities outside of school.
7. Know your campus.
8. Eat your Wheaties!
9. Check your university email.
10. Study.

Written by Eric Faulkes, Jennifer Hockenbery, Gabrielle Matarazzo and Elizabeth Quattrone, who are students at the Robert Busch School of Design, Kean University.

Write Four Enduring Questions

To foster intellectual curiosity and critical thinking, ask questions to wrestle with fundamental issues of human life. The philosopher Socrates advocated discourse in a free community asking enduring (open-ended) questions as a means to pursue wisdom and virtue.

Enduring questions are questions that cross disciplines and have more than one reasonable and interesting answer. The U.S. National Endowment for the Humanities (NEH) states, "Enduring questions can be tackled by reflective individuals regardless of their chosen vocations, areas of expertise, or personal backgrounds." NEH developed the following list of sample questions, which "is neither prescriptive nor exhaustive but serves to illustrate":

- What is good government?
- Can war be just?
- What is friendship?
- What is evil?
- Are there universals in human nature?
- What are the origins of the universe?

Write your own list of at least four enduring questions. Survey friends and relatives about which questions they think are most compelling. Or pose one question and answer it as best you can by researching influential thinkers.

Perhaps this excercise will prompt an idea for a tangible tool, an industrial design solution or unique content for a brand or organization. Assuredly it will get you thinking about the big picture of human existence and your personal journey. Here's one of my favorite questions to get you started: Are humans innately altruistic?

Finish the Statement, "I Wish…"

What do you wish for? Do you have big or modest wishes? Personal or global? Do you wish for personal satisfaction or happiness? Do you wish you could inspire social change for the good? Do you wish you had a doughnut right now, or do you wish for something that could ensure your future?

1. Settle on one wish.
2. Do something with it. Could the wish spark an idea for a story in video or motion graphics or an idea for a new method of communication or transportation? For example, *I wish I could communicate without speaking or typing.* To aid people who couldn't speak due to aphasia or illness, Professor Alan Robbins and his student team invented The Talk Chart, a communication device utilizing icons and the alphabet, in the Design Studio at the Robert Busch School of Design, Kean University, which is used in 2,000 hospitals in the USA.

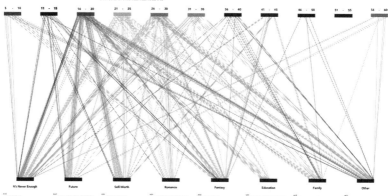

THE 300 WISHES

300 people ranking in a diverse age group were asked their question to see is our wishes change over time. At what age do we get sentimental about our wishes? At what age do we start wishing for a better future for our families than a brighter future for ourselves? According to the group, the age group that contributed the most is the 14–20 year olds. These wishes commonly fall into the greed characteristic. The green characteristic is the most popular of all the wishes especially in the 14–20 year olds. Be it a million wish money, a million dollars, or infinite knowledge, it twice is never enough. Given than random, where the wishes in that category do not fall into any of the other descriptions. The next popular is fantasy. The age group of fantasy ranges from 5 – 60 year olds evenly, no matter how old we are, we still have that inner child that wish to be a super hero, a dragon, or even a cat.

If you could have one wish, what would it be?

POSTER: The 300 Wishes
DESIGNER: Rio R. Venturina © 2014
CREATIVE DIRECTOR: Jennifer Sterling

"This poster is based on a survey of 300 people asking them their one true wish. Each wish is categorized by each type from greed to random and also categorized by the people's ages," says Venturina.

Make the World Better

Dr. Manu Prakash, Assistant Professor of Bioengineering at Stanford University, and his team created a paper microscope, an invention that holds great promise for healthcare in developing countries. Dr. Prakash said, "I build and design tools to uncover how and why biological systems so often outsmart us. I believe one day we will be able to understand the physical design principles of life on Earth, leading to a new way to look at the world we live in."

Can you create a new opportunity through the design, rethinking or repurposing of a material, technology, product, environment or mode of transportation? This is your chance to use your thinking skills and imagination to make the world better.

Turn an idea into a hands-on experiment. Reinvent an existing product or structure by changing materials or extending an existing object's function.

Here are some examples. How about turning a drinking straw into a water filter? "LifeStraw® water filters convert contaminated water into clean, safe drinking water. The easy-to-use filters are a vital tool for some of the 780 million people who don't have ready access to safe drinking water. This leaves them at risk for diarrheal disease, which kills more than 1.5 million people every year. Safe drinking water is especially important for vulnerable groups, such as children under five, pregnant women and people living with HIV" (www.lifestraw.com).

Or what about changing the material of a temporary shelter for the purpose of disaster relief? "Concrete Canvas Shelters are rapidly deployable hardened shelters that require only water and air for construction. A CCS25 variant can be deployed by 2 people without any training in under an hour and is ready to use in only 24 hours. Essentially, Concrete Canvas Shelters are inflatable concrete buildings" (http://www.concretecanvas.com).

Devise a New Use for a Small Ordinary Box

What can you do with one or several small canvas-covered boxes? You could paint it. You could position an assortment of found or made objects inside the box to create a diorama. Could you use the box(es) for a game? Could the boxes conjure memories or fantasies?

Could you trap bad dreams in one, as I proposed in *The Dream Box? The Dream Box* tells the story of Alex, a bird who is determined "to stay awake forever" after he is troubled by a series of bad dreams. When his family's advice to think of "nice things" and have "happy thoughts" fails to do the trick, Alex can barely keep his eyes open in school or at home. Just in time, on his bed he finds a Dream Box that is designed to rid him of nightmares permanently. Figure out an unusual use for the box or boxes; you can't use it for ordinary storage.

(**REMEMBER:** if you utilize your solution as original content or a tool for a branded product, service, social cause or organization, determine if it is on-brand for that brand or entity and would have the potential to resonate with the target audience.)

Reimagine a Use for a Paper Plate

Here's the scenario: Your client owns a warehouse full of ordinary paper plates; however, he doesn't want to sell them as paper plates nor does he want to invest in reconfiguring them. He is hiring you.

Invent a new use for the paper plate.

Your client will sell the paper plate "as is with instructions." You can cut and bend and staple and tape it—do whatever you need to do when thinking, prototyping and testing, but the customer will receive only a paper plate(s) and your instructions with a photograph of the end product. The customer will have to construct whatever you've conceived.

Draw an Encounter on a Coffee Cup

Have a face-to-face conversation or meeting with someone.

Using words and images or only images, record your encounter (conversation, gestures, physical interactions) on a blank coffee cup in a real time variant—where the exact time of the conversation is pretty much equal to the time it takes to view and decipher its depiction on the coffee cup. Or don't worry about real time and just represent the encounter on the cup. Suggest that your companion do it too.

CHILDREN'S PICTURE BOOK SPREADS
FROM: *The Dream Box* by Robin Landa

DESIGN AND ILLUSTRATION:
Modern Dog Design Co.

Running from a ninja frog in his
sleep, Alex fell to the floor.

Staying awake all night listening to
his father's snores was far better than
having that dream again.

"Mom, this time I dreamed about
triple-eyed toads who wanted
to turn me into their dinner!"

"There are neither ninja
frogs nor triple-eyed
toads in this known
universe—I assure you.
Now, try thinking of
nice things to help you
have sweet dreams, my
love. We all have to get
some sleep," Alex's mom
advised patiently.

Think about the narrative as linear or nonlinear. Involve the coffee cup structure, conceiving your narrative either top-down, bottom-up, in horizontal or vertical sections, or in a continuous frieze-like spiral narrative band, as in the Column of Trajan in Rome. On that famous column, the emperor Trajan's military campaigns are commemorated in a continuous narrative; the episodes flow into one another.

Will you commemorate your encounter or document it? Will you have scenes or streams of words and pictures? Will you plan your structure or allow it to happen spontaneously? Will the significance be in the recording, the viewing or both? What can you use this end product for?

(Great thanks to David Haase for suggesting we draw on coffee cups in one of my classes at the Robert Busch School of Design.)

Plan a (Negotiated) Perfect Day

Find a partner. This is fun to do over a meal or coffee. Each of you should plan your perfect day and then share your plan and negotiate a perfect day together.

1. Plan your perfect day on paper.
2. Try your best to convince your partner that he or she should partake in your plans rather than his or her own. Your partner should do the same.
3. Finally you need to come to an agreement.
4. Analyze your planned day for a brand promotion (entertainment, information or tool). The promotion can take any form and you can deliver it across any imagined media channel.
5. Determine if the content would be appropriate for particular products or services, such as tourism for a specific city, a walking shoe, a restaurant chain and so on. Once you determine the product or service category, identify for which specific brand this unique content would be appropriate since different brands within the same category (think footwear, nonalcoholic beverages, travel and tourism, etc.) have different brand personalities.

Create an Authentic Happiness Résumé

What makes you happy?

Does enjoying as many pleasures as possible make you happy?

Does sharing your life with others through friendship, play or love make you happy?

Does serving others or working for the social good make you happy?

Rewrite and redesign your *résumé* to reflect what does or would make you happy in your career and life.

Create for a Neglected Audience

If you think about audience gaps in business sectors or services, you might be able to conceive new products and services.

Where's the gap? Is there a clear gap in a service industry? Is there a gap in the way a current business model operates? Which audience is underserved? Are senior citizens underserved? Can you envision a new kind of nursing home that would modify the current business model? Is there a wide enough variety of computer games aimed at tween girls? Can you conceive a computer game for the visually impaired or a "music experience" for the hearing impaired?

Design a product or service for a neglected audience segment. You can think in terms of demographics (age, gender), psychographic (interests, lifestyles, values), product usage, or community.

Promote Awareness of a Social Issue

You may have had a video-game-filled adolescence. Could you imagine a video game promoting awareness of a social issue for an individual player or for an online collaboration? Or could you connect a game to another cultural medium to promote awareness? Do people pay attention to posters any more? How about outdoor billboards? How could you engage an audience with a poster, object, tool or motion graphic to promote awareness?

Engaging an audience on behalf of a brand is challenging because it's hard to get people to feel something about a product or service. But when you advocate for a cause, you can go for people's guts, appeal to their

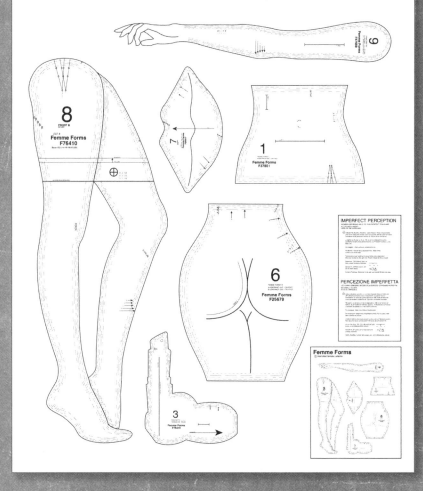

Femme Forms?

POSTER: Femme Forms

DESIGNER: Kaila Edmondson
(© 2014 Kaila Edmondson | All rights reserved.)

CREATIVE DIRECTOR:
Jennifer Sterling

The subject of this poster takes the often emotional aspect of one's body image and views it from a more measured perspective, drawing upon fashion patterns and surgeon's drawn marks on a body. It is a commentary on society's pressure on women to be perfect.

logical sides or both. If you've ever wanted to make a measurable difference in our society, here's a chance to start.

Identify a select number of significant public issues. Then choose one. Call people to action on behalf of that issue through visual communication or a tool.

Think about how you can get people to seriously address a social issue. Make it clear that the source of the conflict is societal. And don't use guilt. Empower people.

> *"I am always doing that which I can not do, in order that I may learn how to do it."* —Pablo Picasso

CHAPTER 03

THINKING ACTIVELY

Knowing how to think empowers you far beyond those who know only what to think. —**NEIL DEGRASSE TYSON**, astrophysicist, Director of the Hayden Planetarium

CRITICAL THINKING

Most everyone would agree that critical thinking is an organized process. Fewer realize efficacious creative thinking is an organized process as well. People who are not in the arts tend to think creativity is unharnessed and spontaneous. They might think the capacity for creative thinking is an inborn golden nugget of genius that only a fortunate population possesses. Those notions are romantic myths. Some people may not even realize that imagination (world-building thinking skills) and creativity are thinking processes! Whether critical or creative, thinking is a purposeful cognitive process.

Here's proof of these thinking processes: In the design disciplines, we use critical and creative thinking to generate ideas that communicate visually and are hopefully beneficial. Furthermore, we use our critical and creative thinking to assess whether those ideas are worth exploring further or are useful.

In a *New York Times* interview titled "How to Get a Job at Google," Laszlo Bock, the head of hiring at Google, told Thomas L. Friedman: "Humans are by nature creative beings, but not by nature logical, structured-thinking beings. Those are skills you have to learn. One of the things that makes people more effective is if you can do both. ... If you're great on both attributes, you'll have a lot more options. If you have just one, that's fine, too." Friedman commented, "But a lot fewer people have this kind of structured thought process *and* creativity."

Critical thinkers *actively* use their intelligence and cognitive skills to take initiative and generate ideas independently. Intelligent concepts drive effective design and advertising. To generate worthy concepts, you must be able to utilize thinking skills in a number of complex ways. To do this, begin by asking investigative questions in order to make informed decisions and achieve goals.

Penetrating Questions

You might be surprised to learn that some designers underuse investigative questions as a means to acquire new knowledge or better understand a given problem. If you've learned to conduct research or you're an innate explorer, you are probably asking many of these questions perhaps without realizing they are integral to a refined reasoning process. To best understand any problem you are undertaking, ask different kinds of penetrating questions.

Rudyard Kipling immortalized the following questions, referring to them in "The Elephant's Child" as "six honest serving men" that taught him all he knew. This set of six *questions of fact* and *analysis* help acquire information necessary to shape informed concepts.

QUESTIONS OF FACT:

- Who?
- What?
- Where?
- When?

QUESTIONS OF ANALYSIS:

- Why?
- How?

You can tailor these six questions into the form of any design brief.

- Who is the audience?
- What is the problem?
- Where does this problem exist?
- When does it happen?
- Why is it happening?
- How can we overcome this problem?

Categories of Questions

The following kinds of questions are loosely based on the original categories of Bloom's Taxonomy. If you pursue the answers, they will help you better understand what you're dealing with and reveal information that can be synthesized into your design research or project context.

KNOWLEDGE (OR FACT) QUESTIONS—GATHER BASIC INFORMATION:

- When does this happen?
- What is an example of this?
- How much is needed? How much is dispensed? Et cetera.
- How often does this occur? How often should we do this? Et cetera.

COMPREHENSION QUESTIONS—UNDERSTAND, INTERPRET, DISTINGUISH, EXTRAPOLATE:

- What does this mean? (Restate a given problem in your own words.)
- What exceptions are there?
- Which part doesn't make sense?

ANALYSIS QUESTIONS—EXAMINE, INVESTIGATE, SCRUTINIZE, BREAK DOWN:

- How does this happen?
- What is the premise?
- What causes this?
- What are the reasons for this? (Scientists examine multiple possibilities and ask this question to elicit a gamut of responses.)
- What evidence is offered? (Scientists can't ignore this question and neither should designers.)

HYPOTHESIS QUESTIONS—EXPLORE THE PREMISE OR PROPOSITION:

- If this happens, then what happens?

- What does this theory predict will happen?

APPLICATION QUESTIONS—PROBLEM SOLVE, RECOGNIZE PATTERNS AND MODELS AND TRANSFER TO NEW OR UNFAMILIAR PROBLEMS:
- What would happen when... ?
- What is the pattern of... and can we apply it to... ?

EVALUATION QUESTIONS—MEASURE AGAINST CRITERIA, ASSESS, STATE WHY:
- Is this effective or ineffective?
- Is it on target? On-brand (in sync with the core brand narrative)? Off-brand (out of sync with the core brand narrative)?
- What fallacies or inconsistencies appear here?
- Is this relevant or irrelevant to our audience?

SYNTHESIS QUESTIONS—CREATE, COMBINE OR INTEGRATE IDEAS TO CREATE A NEW WHOLE:
- How else can we...?
- How can we combine/design these parts into a model/prototype that was not evident before?
- If we integrate X with Y, what will we get?

> *"Science is a way of thinking much more than it is a body of knowledge."*
> —**CARL SAGAN**, astronomer

Employing Active Thinking

When you explore any situation or problem by asking relevant, probing questions and utilizing your brainpower and skills, you are thinking actively. When you examine a variety of concepts and support and consider your conclusions (with evidence), you are thinking independently. When you discuss ideas in an organized fashion with your creative team and view them from your teammates' or from diverse perspectives, you are listening and thinking reflectively.

Examining your own thinking processes—being a meta-thinker—while employing a design discipline-specific approach propels your thinking even further. Focus on how you utilize facts, the rationality of your arguments, making inferences and assumptions, and how you and others draw conclusions.

THINKING ACTIVELY INVOLVES:

- understanding goals
- exploring with questions
- gathering information as raw material
- drawing inferences
- considering necessary points of view
- viewing the problem from different perspectives
- discussing ideas in an organized fashion
- exploring concepts
- refining concepts
- reflecting on the assumptions and consequences of one's thinking
- constructing concepts and solutions

SOLVING PROBLEMS

Problem finding (as explained in chapter 2) prepares you to conduct problem solving. After preparation, to effectively solve a problem, the first step is to define the problem.

- What problem do you need to solve?
- Assess what you know about it.
- What are the parameters of the project?
- Did you explore several possible paths?
- What are the benefits and disadvantages of each path?
- Which possibilities will you pursue?
- Do you need additional information or research in order to proceed?
- What steps do you need to take towards a solution or solutions (alternatives)?
- Have you considered divergent and various points of view?
- Bottom line question: What results do you want?

To achieve efficacy, creatives navigate these kinds of questions, but they don't necessarily process them linearly. Creatives tend towards a more fluid process, integrating methodologies. Making use of these questions leads to a more developed repertoire of intuitive strategies. (Your intuition does develop with knowledge and experience.)

> If you stay open to possibilities, even while realizing a solution, your receptiveness to ideas can suggest paths you hadn't considered.

Goals

Identify the applicable goals. What are you trying to achieve, in the short term and long term? What is the aim of the design or visual communication problem or assignment? Bottom line question to ask yourself: What exactly am I trying to make happen?

Making sure you fully understand the overarching goal and objectives (which are more specific than goals) of the assignment allows you to focus your thinking. If you don't fully understand what you are trying to achieve, you run great risk of going off task.

Restating the problem in your own words helps. Ask questions to aid your comprehension. To realize a fluid creative process, employ an organized thinking process, conduct research, and focus.

Organized Thinking Process
- Identify the goals and objectives.
- Rank them according to importance.
- Focus on the most critical goals and objectives.
- Devise a manageable, actionable plan and strategies to make it happen.
- Manage your steps and time.

Research
Research informs your thinking. It can help you discover an insight that leads to a solid concept. Remember to cross-reference and use reliable

sources. Once you conduct necessary research, gather the information (facts, data, evidence, experiences, testimonies, etc.) and read the material with your audience and goals in mind.

Any solution should be idea-driven rather than media-driven. Once you generate a concept for a brand, group or cause, you then determine the best media channel or mix of channels for dissemination.

> Be aware of any surprising or enlightening bit that points to a solution you hadn't anticipated. That's what makes for good scientific thinking. If you only approach your data looking for something to rationalize a preconceived notion, you aren't discovering but only confirming what you already thought.

Focus

Once you've restated the problem, for the sake of clarity can you be more precise? Precise language clarifies thinking.After reviewing the problem as a whole, break the problem down into smaller parts, if possible, while keeping the whole in mind. Assess whether the smaller parts add meaning or provoke insight.

Breadth, Diversity and Relevance

Look at the problem from the audience's point of view.
- View the problem from other viewpoints—such as topics of interest, age, gender, culture or communities.
- Are you sympathetic to others in your thinking? Make sure your thinking is fair-minded.
- Consult with other kinds of experts or creative team members. Consider others' viewpoints if they can support their arguments.
- Is the emerging central idea significant and relevant?
- Imagine your solution conceptualized for different media channels. How could each rich media experience bring depth to the solution?

Consider the Possibilities Within the Parameters

Contemplate the parameters. Determine what kind of imaginative actions or alternatives are possible given the constraints but don't ignore immutable constraints. For example, if the media is predetermined, you are likely stuck with it. Or if you have budget constraints, those are usually immutable.

Are the boundaries predefined or can you define or redefine them? Would it be advantageous to reinvent the boundaries? What are the alternatives? What can you change? Do you need more information or counsel from other experts to make an informed decision?

> Take care not to mistake as definite those circumstances that are mutable. Circumstances may appear to set up boundaries, but often circumstances can be changed.

Rudimentary Scientific Process

Creative people infuse critical thinking with divergent strategies; however, we all must assess projected project outcomes for efficacy. To do this, to think any problem through, we borrow a basic scientific methodology.

To make discoveries, scientists use this general process:

1. Identify an area for investigation.
2. Gather information to describe the situation as accurately as possible.
3. Develop a hypothesis to explain what is happening.
4. Test the hypothesis through experimentation.
5. Evaluate whether the results confirm or are consistent with the hypothesis.

Similar to the scientific approach, advertising expert Alex Osborn (who created the concept of brainstorming) and Dr. Sidney Parnes developed a process called Osborn-Parnes Creative Problem Solving. It outlines the steps of creative problem solving. Any process such as this one may be employed in a nonlinear fashion. A nonlinear approach allows you to attack any problem in a less predictable way and hopefully challenge conventions.

> "The scientific method helps us understand the nature
> of our world and to test worlds yet unknown. Science is a beguiling,
> demanding, impish lover; the better understood, the more
> lasting, meaningful and rewarding your relationship becomes,
> revealing beauty when you least expect it."
> —JEFFREY H. TONEY, Ph.D., scientist and Provost and
> Vice President for Academic Affairs, Kean University

Osborn-Parne's Creative Problem Solving (CPS):

- Mess finding (or objective finding): identifying the goal, challenge and future direction.
- Fact finding: collecting data about the problem and observing the problem as objectively as possible.
- Problem finding: examining the various parts of the problem to isolate the major part. Make sure you're focusing on the right problem and core aspect of the problem. (Here, problem finding is used differently than presented in chapter 2. Here it means identify the core problem to solve.)
- Idea finding: brainstorming to generate as many ideas as possible regarding the problem .
- Solution finding: developing and selecting criteria to evaluate the solutions and choosing the solution that would be most appropriate.
- Acceptance finding: creating a plan of action.

The Watson-Glaser Critical Thinking Appraisal

The Watson-Glaser Critical Thinking Appraisal measures one's ability to think critically and problem solve by assessing five critical thinking skills: inference, recognition of assumptions, deduction, interpretation and evaluation of arguments.

If you don't examine your conclusions or reflect on your thinking, you run the risk of going with an unsubstantiated premise or design concept. A strong solution is one you can support with reasoning or a rationale.

Critical thinking skills coupled with creative thinking skills enable you to synthesize imagination with information, arriving at well-considered conclusions. To think critically, you must structure a rationale, be able to analyze, synthesize and evaluate information, make inferences and assumptions, and finally be able to draw conclusions that you can support.

Along those lines, ask yourself:

- Did you form a *justified* inference—a conclusion or opinion that follows known facts or evidence?
- Are you aware of your assumptions, ideas you are effectively taking for granted? Are you making unexamined assumptions?
- Are you using the process of deducing—utilizing logic or reason to form a conclusion or opinion?
- Can you distinguish your interpretation from the evidence?
- Can you evaluate the credibility of an argument or rationale?
- Can you analyze whether your argument is valid and assess if your solution is on target, weak or strong?

Discovery consists of looking at the same thing as everyone else and thinking something different.

—**ALBERT SZENT-GYÖRGYI,** physiologist

CHAPTER 4

STORY:
CRAFTING NARRATIVE EXPERIENCES IN THE AGE OF DIGITAL CONTENT

You're never going to kill storytelling, because it's built into the human plan. We come with it.

—MARGARET ATWOOD, author

THE NEW CHALLENGE

Designers have always told stories through visual communications. We tell stories on book covers, in editorial spreads, on posters and through other formats. During World War II, the Rosie the Riveter "We Can Do It!" poster called women to action. A compelling story told through an illustration urged them to contribute to the war effort by joining the work force.

Of course, illustrators, cartoonists, photojournalists, and filmmakers visually communicate stories. In Manohla Dargis's *New York Times* review of the Disney movie *Maleficent*, she wrote, "Mr. Stromberg, a production designer making his feature directing debut, does best when he scales down, as in the lovely shots of Maleficent walking next to a floating, unconscious Aurora, an image that telegraphs more about their relationship than any line of dialogue."

POSTER: Rosie the Riveter:
"We Can Do It!"
ARTIST: J. Howard Miller
COMMISSIONER:
Westinghouse Electric &
Manufacturing Company
DATE: ca. 1942

Today graphic designers and art directors craft narrative brand experiences in ways that are more like short story writers or filmmakers and less like the thinking behind conventional formats—such as concepts for annual reports (thematic; narrative clearly promoting the brand or group) or book covers (that tell a story in the form of a still).

This chapter is not about creating the core brand narrative as a strategic branding premise that sets the foundational brand values and the emotional connection with the audience; however, one needs to understand that aspect of branding. The core brand narrative has to be the point of entry and foundation for all specific stories to keep

> *In the age of connectedness the solution is to create ideas that people want to share.*
>
> —AJAZ AHMED, Founder and CEO of AKQA, co-author of *Velocity*

the brand message relevant, engaging and on track as well as to aid brand resonance.

People's behaviors have changed due to the proliferation of social media, video sharing platforms and other technological changes. We need to respond to those changes and create work that finds them where they spend time and addresses their needs, desires and habits. We need to be concerned with crafting brand stories as visual communication experiences. These stories need to *pull in* an audience rather than *be pushed at* the audience (print, banners, annual reports, TV commercials). We need to be able to create content people will seek out, content they want to view and share, content that they respond to as entertainment or relevant information dissemination rather than conventional marketing. Of course, these new-style brand experiences, services or utilities should support the greater brand narrative and have to be on-brand, most often featuring the brand in the story in subtle but integral ways. Think of BMW films, Burger King's "Subservient Chicken," or Chipotle's "The Scarecrow" and "The Beauty Inside" for Toshiba and Intel: These stories can stand alone to entertain, inform, educate and promote or endear people to a brand.

"The ultimate goal is building the work to get people to want to watch it, to participate in it, to share it. If we don't see that kind of potential in an idea, we don't go with it. Essentially the story will make people want to engage with it," explains PJ Pereira, chief creative officer and cofounder, Pereira & O'Dell, whose agency created "The Beauty Inside." (Read the complete interview with PJ Pereria in chapter 6.)

EFFECTIVE BRAND EXPERIENCES FEATURE:

- **STORYTELLING THAT IS ON-BRAND,** such as IBM's "A Boy and His Atom: The World's Smallest Movie" by Ogilvy New York. To get today's youth to admire scientists the way they admire athletes and actors became IBM's mission. Agency Ogilvy writes, "So they asked us: How do we spread the word about science? Our solution was to make the world's smallest movie. Each frame is made of hundreds of atoms (yes, real atoms), moved to their exact placements by the scientists at IBM Research – Almaden. The frames are combined into an animation, which is now the Guinness World Records ™ record holder for World's Smallest Stop-Motion Film. The scientists themselves made the movie."

- **STORY THROUGH ON-BRAND ACTIONS** The brand or group offers an active experience (an event—in person or online, entertainment, education and more) or offers a service, utility or event to tell its story—for example, sports events sponsored by Red Bull, in place of marketing pushed at people.

> Storytelling and story actions depend upon original content that creates a conversation with the audience, whether in the form of cocreation (audience as cocreator), interactive shareable content or some other kind of fostered participation.

STORYTELLING BY DESIGN

People love stories. In *The Storytelling Animal* Jonathan Gottschall asserts that people are storytelling animals. He writes that we navigate life's social issues through stories. Neuroscience is beginning to reveal why stories move us and make us feel and experience emotions: "Brains on fiction 'catch' the emotions enacted on the page or screen."

Studies have demonstrated that most people's brains are more roused by stories than by information recited plainly. We know people love films, novels, plays, graphic novels, soap operas and bedtime stories—everything that revolves around storytelling. Whatever the form, we know unequivocally that well-told stories pull many people in, even when a brand (commercial or nonprofit) is involved. When a story is *not* well told and a brand is featured (prominently or not, even if it is on-brand), it flops. So let's examine some fundamental principles and effective examples.

Story Basics

Create a situation that involves a conflict that is resolved.

There is a Situation | There is a Conflict | There is a Resolution

Pixar storyboard artist Emma Coats (@LawnRocket) shared Pixar's 22 Rules of Storytelling on Twitter. Rule number four is this story-starting template:

Once upon a time there was _____. Every day, _____. One day _____. Because of that, _____. Because of that, _____, until finally _____.

FOR INSTANCE: Once upon a time there were two brothers. Every day the older brother would bully the younger brother. One day the younger brother decided he would fight back. Because of that, the younger brother started lifting weights, until finally his new muscle power intimidated his older brother and the bullying ceased.

A story needs a main direction (often called a *throughline*) and the main character needs a goal. The main direction of the story is all about the character and his/her goal. The goal is either conceived by the character (character driven) or the goal is pushed upon the character by the plot (plot driven), but either way it is still the character's goal.

If you focus on the relationships of the characters, plot will start to fall into place. In *Story Structure Architect: A Writer's Guide to Building Dramatic Situations and Compelling Characters*, Victoria Lynn Schmidt explains the ways the goal of a story can play out.

- The main character succeeds.
- The main character is defeated.
- The main character abandons his or her goal.
- The main character's goal is undefined.
- The viewer creates the goal.

When the audience is involved, let's say on Facebook, an audience member can push the goal upon the character to direct the plot. To further build buzz for an already effective campaign for Old Spice, the "Smell Like a Man, Man—the Sequel" campaign invited consumers to submit questions via Twitter and Facebook to be answered personally by the Old Spice Guy. More than two thousand people sent questions and in a forty-eight-hour period, nearly two hundred personalized video responses were created and posted to YouTube—including videos responding to Ashton Kutcher, Alyssa Milano, and ABC anchor George Stephanopoulos. As a result, Old Spice set new benchmarks for consumer engagement and sparked another viral hit. (Find out more at www.pg.com/en_US/downloads/innovation/factsheet_OldSpice.pdf.)

> *A special effect without a story is a pretty boring thing.*
>
> —GEORGE LUCAS

You can structure a story in a number of ways depending on the context and delivery channel. Interactive channels lend themselves to nonlinear structures. Some structures work best for certain types of content. For example, if you're focusing on a heroic character, a journey structure makes sense. There are traditional structures (following a traditional three-act story structure), such as melodrama or episodic as well as unconventional models, such as metafiction or interactive fiction.

Beyond structure, storytellers harness the power of situations. Ambition, disaster, flawed judgment, obstacles to love, pursuit of a dream or self-sacrifice are conventional dramatic situations that create conflict. There are several main types of conflict—an opposition of forces between people, ideas, natural or manmade circumstances:

- relational conflict (person against person)
- situational conflict (person against nature)
- inner conflict (person against the self)

WHAT'S YOUR BEST ADVICE ABOUT STORYTELLING?

by Steven Doloff, Ph.D., Pratt Institute, Distinguished Professor, Humanities & Media Studies

Hey, You're a Story!

I frame my world literature survey course with the basic idea of Joseph Campbell's classic text on mythology, *The Hero with a Thousand Faces:* perennially popular stories draw on a universal repertoire of archetypal narrative models that all humans are genetically predisposed to respond to and recognize themselves in.

From this self-recognition factor in stories, I draw the corollary proposition that each student's conscious sense of his or her own personal identity is *itself* a constantly unfolding and reformulating story that each tells him- or herself on a regular basis, as a way of knowing and reaffirming who they are in the world. Their story is their self-recognition through time.

My students may initially feel that their identity-stories are foisted upon them by chance, circumstance or other people. But I propose to them that, in a humanistic sense, they have the power to assume increasing authorship over their own identity-stories by broadening their awareness of the many possible storylines they can choose (or construct) to shape how they see themselves.

This broadening process is a mixture of (1) the critical analysis of the material, social and political conditions they already find impacting them, and (2) the active pursuit of new and unfamiliar experiences and ideas to discover the infinitely rich and strange potential for what their identity-stories can become.

My purpose in this class is to convince my students that the deeper they can look into *The Epic of Gilgamesh* or *Candide* or *Mrs. Dalloway*, the deeper they can look into themselves. This class is a requirement for Pratt Institute's Writing Program majors, and my opening words to them are: "You can't *write* a story until you can read one."

- paranormal conflict (person against technology or magical or supernatural force)
- cosmic conflict (person against destiny or person against an omnificent force or universal forces)
- social conflict (person against a group/society)

STORY EXERCISES

» In fifty words or less, tell us about a conflict you have with a friend, family member or significant other.

» In six words, describe something you see almost every day on your way to work or school.

» Picture the door of a room in a legendary hotel, such as the Hotel Chelsea in Manhattan where famous musicians stayed. What stories do you find behind the door?

Examples of Effective Storytelling

Documentary Film: "From One Second to the Next"
CLIENT: AT&T
AGENCY: BBDO

Created for AT&T's "It Can Wait" campaign, this thirty-five-minute documentary film, directed by Werner Herzog, looks at the lives of four people impacted by texting-while-driving accidents. This film and the documented individuals were featured in the campaign's television spots, also directed by Herzog.

"Among the subjects of the film are Xzavier, a young boy who was left paralyzed by a car accident caused by texting, and Chandler Gerber, who killed three people while reading a text behind the wheel of a van. … [The film is] intelligently shot and produced, but at times can be very difficult to watch. Chandler Gerber's vivid account of the accident he caused is particularly harrowing. ... The documentary is being distributed to over 40,000 high schools" (www.wernerherzog.com).

Short Film: "Put on a Smile"—The Wearable Movie

CLIENT: The Coca-Cola Company
AGENCY: Ogilvy & Mather New York

The short film is about a pair of friends who attempt to make giant lips smile. Each frame of the animated short was printed on an individual T-shirt. The Coca-Cola company sent hundreds of these shirts to staff, creative partners and social media fans all over the world with a thank you note, asking these folks to upload a photo of themselves wearing the shirt. One hundred percent of the people participated. The frames were cobbled together to create the first "wearable movie."

Package Design: Sharing Can

CLIENT: The Coca-Cola Company
AGENCY: Ogilvy & Mather Singapore and Ogilvy Paris

To continue their story of sharing happiness for Coca-Cola, Ogilvy asked, *What if people could share the actual can itself?* After pooling resources and thinking, Ogilvy & Mather Singapore and Ogilvy & Mather France designed a can that could be twisted, turned and shared (one can of Coke becomes two separate sealed cans of Coke), delivering another part of the happiness-sharing story. (See more at www.coca-colacompany.com/stories/coke-for-2-sharing-can-doubles-the-happiness.)

Interactive: Nature Valley Trail View

CLIENT: General Mills/Nature Valley
AGENCY: McCann Erickson New York

This project is a virtual hike through U.S. national parks. According to the Interpublic Group,"[It's] a first-of-its-kind interactive experience that allows visitors on NatureValleyTrailView.com to virtually hike the trails of the Grand Canyon, Yellowstone, and the Great Smoky Mountains.

"To capture 360-degree footage of nearly 60 trails, the team hiked 333 miles over three months...The effort began when the creative directors imagined applying Google Street View-style technology to hiking trails. Nature Valley is a long-standing supporter of America's national parks and this unprecedented digital platform allowed the granola bar maker to create a new brand experience" (www.interpublic.com).

Event: The Double Loop Dare at the X Games
CLIENT: Hot Wheels
AGENCY: Mistress

As part of the "Hot Wheels for Real" campaign, two drivers, Tanner Foust and Greg Tracy, set a Guinness World Record with a life-sized Hot Wheels–like track at the X Games in Los Angeles. To appeal to boys of all ages, Hot Wheels created this event as part of an episodic story with real characters, stunts and a double loop. "The drivers had to hit a speed between 48 mph and 52 mph and the cars were outfitted with extra-stiff suspension and the tires were inflated to 80 psi—60 percent more than normal" (http://mashable.com/2012/07/02/hot-wheels-double-loop).

"Mistress developed TV ads and digital and long-form content surrounding a life-size Hot Wheels jump and world-record attempt at the 100th anniversary celebration of the Indianapolis 500. Following the event, Hot Wheels presented a 30-minute TV special on ABC (and ESPN globally) showcasing the world-record attempt" (http://adage.com/article/small-agency-awards/mistress-ad-age-s-2011-small-agency-1-10-employees-gold/229103).

Story Through Actions
There are some brands that build an action model into their core values and strategy.

"In 2006, TOMS founder Blake Mycoskie befriended children in a village in Argentina and saw that they didn't have adequate shoes to protect their feet. Wanting to help, he created TOMS Shoes, a company that would match every pair of shoes purchased with a pair of new shoes for a child in need. One for One." In 2011, the One for One model was expanded and

TOMS Eyewear was launched. With every pair purchased, TOMS helps restore sight to a person in need. One for One." (Find out more at www.toms.com/one-for-one-en.)

Not Impossible Labs is "a global web-based community of people who pool knowledge and resources to create technology" (www.facebook.com/notimpossiblelabs). The group "utilizes crowd-sourcing to crowd-solve previously insurmountable healthcare issues." Each of their projects "tells the story of a single individual." By focusing on helping one person, they believe they can help many others. By focusing on one problem, they believe they can help solve residual problems. For example, The Chad Cane is "a super cane that integrates laser and sonar technology to provide feedback to the user about their surroundings. This cane will employ both auditory and sensory signals to alert blind individuals to changes in terrain and upcoming obstacles. Ideally, it will also integrate iPhone/Google Maps functionality to notify the user of their location." The Chad Cane team's leader is Javed Gangjee. (Find out more at www.notimpossiblelabs.com.)

Online retailer Zappos' story action is based on how important customer service is to people. Zappos.com states, "Customer Service Isn't Just A Department! We've been asked by a lot of people how we've grown so quickly, and the answer is actually really simple… We've aligned the entire organization around one mission: to provide the best customer service possible. Internally, we call this our WOW philosophy." Rather than simply pushing marketing messages at people, Zappos uses customer-service based actions to support its brand narrative and make their customers' transactions easier.

In his book, *True Story: How to Combine Story and Action to Transform Your Business*, Ty Montague, Cofounder, Co-CEO of co:collective, writes about Storydoing™ —"a public project to delve in to the performance differences between storytelling companies and storydoing companies" (www.story-doing.com/welcome).

He explains the primary characteristics of storydoing companies.

1. They have a story.

2. The story is about a larger ambition to make the world or people's lives better.
3. The story is understood and cared about by senior leadership outside of marketing.
4. That story is being used to drive tangible action throughout the company: product development, HR policies, compensation, etc.
5. These actions add back up to a cohesive whole.
6. Customers and partners are motivated to engage with the story and are actively using it to advance their own stories."

(Find out more at http://blogs.hbr.org/2013/07/ good-companies-are-storyteller)

Examples of Effective Stories through Actions

Sustainable Package Design: Ocean Plastic
CLIENT: Method
DESIGN: Method

Rather than manufacture new plastic, Method's employees and local Hawaiian volunteer groups hand collected plastic on the beaches of Hawaii to reuse, which means less demand for virgin materials and a cleaner Hawaii. The gray color of the package was a natural result after the plastic chopping, washing and pelletizing process.

"As a small soap company, we know we can't clean up the world's oceans. But we can raise awareness about the issue and use our business to demonstrate smart ways of using and reusing the plastics that are already on the planet. We think the best way to do that is by proving that solutions exist, even at a small scale." (Read the entire case study at http://methodhome.com/beyond-the-bottle/ocean-plastic/.)

3D Printing: Project Daniel
CLIENT: Not Impossible Labs
AGENCY: The Ebeling Group and Not Impossible Labs

Not Impossible's Project Daniel uses 3D printers to make prosthetic arms for children of war in South Sudan. "14 year old Daniel Omar was tending his family's cows in the Nuba Mountains of South Sudan when bombs were released overhead. He jumped behind a tree for cover, wrapping his arms around its trunk. The bomb landed a few yards away. While the tree trunk protected Daniel's body, the explosion tore his hands off. ... With an estimated 50,000 amputees in South Sudan, the ongoing conflicts take a massive toll on the region. By helping Daniel regain his independence, Not Impossible aims to empower the local community, and rebuild confidence in its people." (www.notimpossiblelabs.com/#!project-daniel/c1imu)

The project came to fruition at Not Impossible HQ in Venice, California, by crowdsourcing a dream team of innovators (including the South African inventor of the Robohand, an Australian MIT neuroscientist and a 3D printing company owner from Northern California) to crowd-solve the 3D printable prostheses. Not Impossible CEO and founder Mick Ebeling set up what is probably the world's first 3D-printing prosthetic lab and training facility in Sudan's Nuba Mountains.

Online Game: Scrabble Wi-Fi

CLIENT: Scrabble
AGENCY: Ogilvy Paris

Want to brush up on your spelling skills? Can't get on the Internet? Scrabble can help. To gain relevance in a gaming world, Ogilvy Paris created Scrabble Wi-Fi, which turns correct words in the game into passwords for free Wi-Fi access. To promote the game, Ogilvy Paris placed Wi-Fi hotspots in Paris where one couldn't get an Internet connection. If you proved your spelling smarts, you could get connected—the higher the Scrabble score, the longer the connection.

Cedric Geuret, Executive Creative Director of Ogilvy Paris said, "Our objective was simple: to excite people about Scrabble again by getting them to playfully interact with the brand on-the-go via their mobile phones and to demonstrate and remind people the value of knowing how to spell words and rewarding them."

Website: Strong & Kind

Kevin Durant, the forward for the NBA's Oklahoma City Thunder, part-
nered with KIND, a snack food company, to demonstrate "the best way to
show strength is to choose kindness." As part of the initiative, KIND has
donated $1 million to the Kevin Durant Charity Foundation "to create
specialized education and after-school programming for at-risk youth to
teach them to be STRONG and KIND."

Durant and KIND (www.strongandkind.com) ask people to pledge to:

- have the courage to be kind when others may not.
- look out for those who can't look out for themselves.
- stand up when others would rather stand out.
- leave [their] world a kinder place than they found it.
- be strong and kind.

Identity Design: Jewish Museum

CLIENT: Jewish Museum
STUDIO: Sagmeister & Walsh

The Jewish Museum is located in a beautiful seven-story mansion on
Manhattan's Upper East Side. It is the preeminent museum in the United
States devoted to Jewish art and culture. Sagmeister & Walsh's rebranding
of the museum tells a relevant story based on an ancient geometric system.

Sagmeister & Walsh explain, "Our goal in rebranding the museum
was to connect the historic and contemporary, and engage multiple visi-
tor generations. The new identity system we created is founded on 'sa-
cred geometry,' an ancient geometric system from which the Star of David
was formed. The entire branding system is drawn on this grid, from the
word and logo mark, to dozens of patterns, icons, typography, and illus-
trations. To address photography as part of the system, we built a processing app that turns a photo or webcam stream into a Jewish Museum illustration. ... This system invites surprise and flexibility across all media,
while always unified in visual language." (See interview with Jessica Walsh
of Sagmeister & Walsh in chapter 6.)

Content

Looking for a recipe? How about baby-care tips? Or help with your hair? Many brands publish dedicated websites to help answer your questions. The L'Oreal Group publishes Makeup.com. American Express offers OPEN Forum. General Mills publishes Tablespoon.com to share recipes with consumers while marketing their products. A recipe for a sweet potato pie that used Pillsbury piecrust in an unconventional way was a hit with readers, and as a result it intensified General Mills' presence on social media.

What kind of branded content do people seek out online? What kind of content do they share? If content is relevant, interesting, useful or entertaining and the marketing isn't glaring, people will look for it and even pass it along, especially if they think their friends will find it as funny, cool or informative as they do. Designer Josh Owen advises, "Designers must now more than ever have the ability to be curators of content and to be capable of thinking beyond their bag of skills." Whether it's curated content, unique entertainment with or without a message, or some kind of utility, cultivating your knowledge in a variety of subjects will help you generate ideas.

As Mark Avnet, Dean of 360iU, advises: "Really easy: Start with people. Always start with people. What do they need? What are they trying to do in their lives? Then look at the brand. What does it have to offer that might help people do whatever they're trying to do? Does it have the cultural authority to offer that to a particular audience? If so, what creative things can we do, knowing what's possible from a technological standpoint, that will connect people and the brand?" (Read the interview with Avnet in chapter 6.)

The excellent aspect of Dove's Real Beauty Sketches (http://realbeautysketches.dove.us) is how well the creative team understood what is relevant to their audience. To generate an idea like this one, one must have an understanding of what a social experiment is and know about contemporary women's self-images. Dove explains, "Women are their own worst beauty critics. Only four percent of women around the world consider themselves beautiful. At Dove, we are committed to creating a world where beauty is a source of confidence not anxiety. So we decided to conduct a compelling social experiment that explores how women view their own beauty in contrast to what others see. And don't forget: YOU are more beautiful than you think!"

Want to watch Jean-Claude Van Damme do an epic split between moving trucks? Lots of folks do and have watched it over and over again. "The Epic Split" was viewed on YouTube more than 68 million times. It is part of a series of films promoting new Volvo trucks. The film highlights innovative steering technology. And not only can you watch it on YouTube, but you can catch this film at the Musée de la Publicité at the Palais du Louvre in Paris.

Lots of people also delighted in watching cartoon characters find ill-advised ways to die in a three-minute dark humor song and video, "Dumb Ways to Die" (http://dumbwaystodie.com) created by McCann Melbourne for Metro Trains Melbourne, cited previously in chapter 1. Rather than deliver a somber public service ad, McCann Melbourne Executive Creative Director John Mescall said, "Pretty early on, we decided we'd try to create entertainment rather than advertising. For the simple reason that we figured if traditional PSAs repel people, then we should really try to create one that attracts them. ...It was the counterintuitive nature of the idea, the weirdness and positivity of the execution, the sheer joy of the song and the video, and the attention to detail across all elements of the work that ensured its success."

MOTION GRAPHICS

Some designers hold to the idea that if it's not moving, it's dead. Motion graphics go back to early cinematic experiments and experiences. Think of Oskar Fischinger's "Space Light Art" ("Raumlichtkunst") multiple-screen film events, first shown in Germany in 1926; or the innovative use of techniques by Norman McLaren, such as paper cutouts ("Rythmetic," codirected by Evelyn Lambart, 1956; "Le Merle," 1958) or animating a chalk drawing ("Là-Haut Sur Ces Montagnes," 1945). Saul Bass and Pablo

Ferro made indelible impressions on graphic design with their motion graphic works.

Motion graphics play a significant role across devices—whether on a small mobile screen or a huge public screen and every size in between. Sound and movement aid storytelling. With motion, you can show (rather than tell) more easily. You can make complicated accounts or demonstrations much more plain with motion.

INTEGRATING MOTION INTO STORYTELLING:

- The motion serves the storytelling and propels it. What is the purpose of the story's motion? Write the purpose in one or two sentences.
- The final rule of Emma Coats' "Pixar's 22 Rules of Storytelling" is critical: "What's the essence of your story? Most economical way of telling it? If you know that, you can build out from there."
- Pre-production, work out the story structure and map out the motion.
- How will the journey look?
- Figure out the ending first; it gives you direction.
- Move the drama or story forward. Keep the audience's attention at all times. Contrast, texture, pattern, changes in scale, and visual surprise help.
- Apply the major design principles to the motion graphics: balance, visual hierarchy, unity and especially rhythm. Utilize a storyboard to plan the rhythm of the journey.
- Consider establishing a dominant color in your color palette.
- Use sound to move the story along and for emphasis and expression.
- Edit and revise for fluidity and brevity. Streamline.
- Determine if the story works for the media channel and whether it is a linear or nonlinear context and delivery.

In six panels, tell the story of a brief encounter between a duck and dog.

CHAPTER 5

STAYING NIMBLE

*People talk about change and adaptation, but they
don't see how fast the competition is coming, from everywhere.
We have to move. We have no choice.*

—**BOB GREENBERG**, CEO and Founder of R/GA

FAST & FEARLESS

Staying nimble requires play, observation, listening, reflection, lifelong learning and taking things in stride—a kind of bravery. It requires becoming—an active habitual process (what choreographer Twyla Tharp calls "the creative habit")—and a lifestyle approach to developing your cognitive and creative abilities.

Play

What do IDEO, Google and children have in common? Play. Dr. Peter Gray, Research Professor, Psychology, Boston College, explains:

> Play, by definition, is what we *want* to do as opposed to what we feel compelled to do. Adult "work" is playful to the degree that adults enjoy it. Sociologists studying employment satisfaction have found that the qualities of a job that lead to most satisfaction are those qualities that make the work playful—autonomy (freedom to choose how and when

to do the work, no micromanagement by bosses), creativity (the work could not be done by a robot), and challenge (play is never easy, because when it is easy it becomes boring and is no longer play).

(Please see the complete interview with Dr. Gray in chapter 6.)

Many designers play through an exploration of materials, as did the famous husband and wife design team of Charles and Ray Eames. To prepare students for specialized studies, the Bauhaus preliminary course immersed them in the study of materials along with color theory and composition. Josef Albers, esteemed artist and educator, who taught at the Bauhaus, Yale University and Black Mountain College, believed his goal as an educator was "to open eyes." In *Teaching Form Through Practice* (http://albersfoundation.org/teaching/josef-albers/texts) he wrote:

> I get ideas by observing people and how
> they live. It helps me develop ideas of what people need,
> what they wish the future would bring them.
>
> —YVES BÉHAR, designer

Inventive construction and an attentiveness that leads to discoveries are developed—at least initially—through experimentation that is undisturbed, independent, and thus without preconceptions. This experimentation is (initially) a playful tinkering with the material for its own sake. That is to say, through experimentation that is amateurish (i.e. not burdened by training) ...

Experimentation skips over study and a playful beginning develops courage. Thus we do not begin with a theoretical introduction: at the beginning there is *only* the material, if possible without tools. This procedure leads naturally to independent thinking and the development of an individual style.

LET'S PLAY

When children play, they don't worry. But adults worry about appearing foolish or taking missteps. Children rarely apologize for being silly or

> *In play you don't foresee an end product.*
> *It allows you to suspend judgment. Often the solution to*
> *one problem sparks a possibility for another set of problems.*
> *Sometimes that happens in the process of building a work.*
> **—RICHARD SERRA**, artist

saying something zany or taking an invented game in a fantastical or odd direction. They go with their flow. Adults are often too self-conscious to play with abandon.

When you do take some time during your day to participate in creative play, don't worry about anything. Enjoy yourself and let your thinking flow. And if it makes you feel better, remind yourself that it will improve your skills.

Play is what you *want* to do so as opposed to what you're told to do, so it may seem counterintuitive to offer exercises. But if you would like a way to begin (which can be the most challenging part), here are starters that have proven very effective with hundreds of students.

Unconventional Tools

Use unconventional drawing tools, materials and methods. For instance, draw with a squeeze bottle filled with nontoxic liquid fabric dye or liquid soap, a paint-dipped badminton shuttlecock of feathers, or coffee cup rings. Create a drawing that challenges conventions or your own notions about visual art.

Beauty of Chance

Place a big piece of paper on your desk or the floor. Tear up other pieces of paper. Drop them on the big page, then adhere them to the page just as they fell. Draw around, over and next to them. Draw automatically as it comes to you, without premeditated concerns.

Decalcomania

Apply black India ink or paint to a piece of paper. Then press that paper against another surface, transferring an image that results in a fractal pattern. Expound on the visual when dry or work into it when wet.

From Organic to Geometric

On graph paper, begin with a random spill or blot of India ink. Extending out from the free form spill, develop the image into geometric shapes and forms—that's where the graph paper becomes a guide. Don't think about it too much: just draw.

Make a Mess

Work with a brush loaded with India ink or black acrylic paint to make any kind of large shapes. Generate drips, splashes and long broad brushstrokes.

Free Drawing

Start each day with twenty minutes of free drawing. Draw anything that comes to mind. If you find a blank page daunting, start with a curved line or a random shape and go from there.

Tangle Doodle

On a page, draw a continuous line that intersects at several points. The intersections should result in compartmental closed shapes. Within each compartment, draw a different pattern. A black fine-point marker or a 2B pencil is good for this.

Photo-Editing Software

Scan a photograph of someone you dislike and import it into photo-editing software. Rotate one feature on the face. Evaluate the change. Then do whatever you like.

Self-Portrait

Scan a photograph of yourself and import it into photo-editing software. Duplicate the photo. Now you have two of you. Find an interesting way to connect the two images.

Textures

Find pairs of very different textures. Juxtapose them in pairs to create the most contrast or pair them to jump-start a story.

Homage to Josef Albers

Find some newspapers. Take the newspaper you have and "make something out of it which is more than it is now." (Reported by Hannes Beckmann in *Die Gründerjahre.*)

Sharpening Listening Skills

Using a notebook or drawing pad or tablet and drawing tool, take sketch notes or written notes while listening to an extended conversation. Listen for key words and for understanding. Summarize in a sketch and phrase of six words or fewer.

Take a Line For a Walk

Draw a line and see where it takes you. Start a line on another page so that you have a place to start drawing the next day. (Author Richard Nochimson always ends his daily writing session by beginning a passage he can pick up during the next session. That way, he can jump right in when he starts writing the next day.)

> *I sometimes begin drawing with no preconceived problem to solve, with only a desire to use pencil on paper and only to make lines, tones and styles with no conscious aim... But as my mind takes in what is so produced a point arrives where some idea becomes conscious and crystallizes, and then control and ordering begin to take place.*
>
> **—HENRY MOORE,** artist

Let's Play Another Way

Posing *What if...?* questions is guaranteed to jump-start your imagination and enhance your creative thinking. It might even inspire you to try to change the world one idea at a time.

Here are some questions with far-reaching consequences.

WHAT IF kicking a soccer ball could generate power to light a bulb? (A question that generated SOCCKET, the "energy-harnessing soccer ball," by http://unchartedplay.com.)

WHAT IF hypertext could facilitate sharing and updating information among researchers? (This query solved by Tim Berners-Lee, Director of the World Wide Web Consortium.)

WHAT IF you could move heavy objects on hardened ice paths slicked with water? (A method used in fifteenth-century China to construct the Forbidden City.)

WHAT IF you mix flour, water and yeast together? (The world would have been deprived of leavened bread if people didn't ask this question.)

WHAT IF...? questions might prompt follow-up questions. For example, if one asked, "What if we could become invisible at will?" follow-up questions could then include: What's the advantage to being invisible? When would you want to be invisible? What are examples of when it would be good to be invisible and when it would be bad to be invisible? How could we make it possible for someone to become invisible?

What if...

- there were a storage device for all your memories?
- you could undo one bad thing in history?
- you could print an artificial limb from a 3D printer? (Mick Ebeling's idea for Project Daniel at Not Impossible Labs.)
- there were twenty-seven letters in the alphabet?
- we could make temporary shelters that could resist rough winds?
- professional baseball included women?
- everyone recycled?
- you found out your mayor is planning to...?
- there were a drinking straw that filters out impurities in water? (The inspiration for LifeStraw®.)
- no one ever died?
- your parents could choose your talent?

- you could invent a new way to communicate with another person?
- everyone turned the other cheek?
- at age ten you had to pick your best friend for life?
- we could easily travel through outer space?

IF ONLY… works as a lead-in statement to prompt imaginative thoughts as well. This starter embeds a wish or desire of some kind that could lead to realizing what tools, apps or services a brand or organization could provide for an audience.

If only …

- my car could drive itself. (The inspiration for autonomous vehicles.)
- I could grow another head to solve hard problems.
- my skills were like those of James Bond.
- my voice could change unrecognizably at will.
- there were 3D-printed steel construction joints that could be used to create more efficient structures. (A statement that inspires the engineering firm Arup).
- I could disguise myself daily.
- everyone could have access to locally-grown fresh food.
- you could issue private currency. (The inspiration for Bitcoin.)

On his website, neilgaiman.com, author Neil Gaiman answers a question he is often asked: Where do you get your ideas? First he tells people that he makes ideas up in his head; then he says he uses "What if…" and "If only…" questions. He continues:

> And then there are the others: *I wonder* … ("I wonder what she does when she's alone …") and *If this goes on* … ("If this goes on telephones are going to start talking to each other, and cut out the middleman.") and *Wouldn't it be interesting if* … ("Wouldn't it be interesting if the world used to be ruled by cats?")
>
> Those questions, and others like them, and the questions they, in their turn, pose ("Well, if cats used to rule the world, why don't they any more? And how do they feel about that?") are one of the places ideas come from.

Synthesizing

What if…? questions fit into the cognitive domain of synthesis, a cognitive process involving integrating or combining ideas, experiences or knowledge to generate a new whole, a new pattern or a unique or imaginative way to solve problems or generate concepts. Synthesis is one of the cognitive domains outlined in the original version of Bloom's taxonomy; in the revised version of Bloom's taxonomy, synthesis is called *creating*.

Some key words used in synthesis questions or actions are *design, compose, combine, rearrange, revise, integrate, maximize, minimize, change, invent, juxtapose* and *modify*.

Some key questions to ask are:

- How could these form a new whole?
- If you combine x and y, then you might get …
- If you change this aspect, what would have to happen?
- What would happen if …?
- Suppose you could …?
- What is a possible alternative to …?
- How can you modify this to …?
- Can you construct a model that would change …?
- If you modify this part, what would happen?
- If you integrate this with that, what would the result be?

French mathematician Jacques Hadamard explored how mathematicians invent new ideas. To do so he considered the creative experiences of some of the greatest thinkers of his generation, such as Claude Lévi-Strauss and Albert Einstein. His findings about mental processes in invention in *An Essay on the Psychology of Invention in the Mathematical Field* apply to many forms of creativity. In a letter to Hadamard, Einstein analyzed his own thought process and stressed what he called "combinatory play": "[T]aken from a psychological viewpoint, this combinatory play seems to be the essential feature in productive thought—before there is any connection with logical construction in words or other kinds of signs which can be communicated to others." Conceptual synthesis can lead to ideas, the (vague) combining of bits—elements, images, knowledge, perceptions, and more—with the "desire to arrive finally at logically connected concepts" (Einstein).

To initiate visual or conceptual synthesis, apply action verbs to whatever you've created or any idea you've generated:

- Combine
- Modify
- Reverse
- Amplify
- Twist
- Turn
- Tear

Alfred North Whitehead wrote, "We must beware of what I call 'inert ideas'—ideas that are merely received into the mind without being utilized, or tested, or thrown into fresh new combinations." Keen thinkers combine ideas or objects and habitually make astute observations in order to generate ideas. Many of us have "inert ideas;" deliberately making use of them is an excellent daily practice. What makes a creative thinker is the ability to utilize or propel those inert ideas into fresh combinations. To do this one must learn about subjects outside of one's area of expertise and practice active observation. Learn to focus and be mindful enough to turn your synthetic cognitive process into executable value creation.

> *To know one thing, you must know the opposite.*
>
> **—HENRY MOORE**, artist

- Consider the possible results and consequences of doing something.
- Reflect on how the context affects the design experience or meaning.
- Take into account how changing the context would change the outcome.
- Predict an opposite solution or scenario.
- Employ a deletion scenario: What if there were no ...?
- Ask yourself if you'd share or talk about what you just conceived or produced.

Thinking and the Aha Insight

John Kounios (Department of Psychology, Drexel University) and Mark Beeman (Department of Psychology, Northwestern University) examine that moment of insight that solves a problem, resolves an ambiguity or reinterprets a situation. Their article, "The Aha! Moment: The Cognitive Neuroscience of Insight" in the *Current Directions in Psychological Science* journal, explains that what seems like a disconnected flash of insight actually is connected to a series of brain processes. They explain that recently "a series of studies have used electroencephalography (EEG) and functional magnetic resonance imaging (fMRI) to study the neural correlates of the 'Aha! Moment' and its antecedents. Although the experience of insight is sudden and can seem disconnected from the immediately preceding thought, these studies show that insight is the culmination of a series of brain states and processes operating at different time scales. Elucidation of these precursors suggests interventional opportunities for the facilitation of insight."

If you can train yourself to pay attention to how you're thinking creatively, solving a problem or problem finding, you'll be more likely to notice the connections between the insight and the prior thinking and thereby be more likely to replicate a fruitful aha process. To enhance your ability

> *Creativity is just connecting things. When you ask creative people how they did something, they feel a little guilty because they didn't really do it, they just saw something. It seemed obvious to them after a while. That's because they were able to connect experiences they've had and synthesize new things. And the reason they were able to do that was that they've had more experiences than other people.*
>
> —STEVE JOBS

to think on the fly and be nimble, practice mindfulness while you're thinking, designing and working. It pays off.

DAILY EXERCISE

When you're in the act of an everyday activity—waiting in line to pay, riding the bus, having coffee in a café—take written or visual note of one or two ordinary behaviors. What do people do when they're waiting in line? What do people do on the bus? Is anyone talking? How does someone unwrap a packaged good? How does someone chew gum or eat a snack or listen to music?

Personal By Design

According to Dr. Martin E.P. Seligman, who cofounded the field of positive psychology, we can experience three kinds of happiness: 1) pleasure and gratification, 2) embodiment of strengths and virtues, and 3) meaning and purpose. The pleasant life brings positive emotions, but applying and developing one's strengths and virtues in the service of something larger than oneself—in pursuit of a meaningful life—is more likely to bring long-term happiness.

Similarly, investing oneself in creative work yields a greater sense of meaning and happiness. Investing oneself in creative work for clients can

Image No. 203 from
© Jennifer Sterling Design series

DESIGNER: Jennifer Sterling,
Jennifer Sterling Design
(jennifersterlingdesign.com)

be very gratifying. Some designers find further satisfaction in personal projects—what some call "passion projects." And some designers, such as Jennifer Sterling, are *continually* creating because that's what fulfills them.

Independent projects are personal by design. An intense interest in a subject or the act of doing something daily can spark a project. There are no client constraints; no client's watchful eyes. An independent project allows you an independent lens, to do what you want, explore and experiment. It certainly keeps your thinking fresh.

Two good friends, designers Jessica Walsh and Timothy Goodman, "with opposite relationship problems found themselves single at the same time. As an experiment, they dated for 40 days" and created a blog called Forty Days of Dating (http://fortydaysofdating.com). Warner Bros. acquired the screen rights. (See the full interview with Jessica Walsh in chapter 6.)

Peruvian-born designer and illustrator Denyse Mitterhofer stared at her closet full of clothes one day and thought, *I don't have anything to wear!* She suddenly realized that she was taking things for granted—from her morning coffee to the safety she enjoys living in the USA. She decided to celebrate the things she enjoys by making a list of the things she takes for granted and turning that list into a series of posters: "The Things I Take For Granted." Her goal was to remind herself and inspire others. She won an award from *HOW* magazine for the poster series.

Other designers take up other visual art forms in addition, such as sculpture, furniture design, photography, painting, or filmmaking. Pentagram partner Paula Scher paints and exhibits her work. Seymour Chwast, a founding partner of Push Pin Studios, has had several one-man shows of his paintings, sculptures and prints.

Often personal projects take the form of sketchbooks or journals. Some people commit to a sketch a day for a year or more. Designer and illustrator Stefan G. Bucher created the Daily Monster website (www.dailymonster.com). For one hundred days, Bucher filmed himself "putting a few drops of ink on a piece of paper... and transforming the resulting blot into a new monster." Every night, he posted the result on his website and "stood back in wonder as visitors from all over the world told me the amazing stories behind each creature." From this independent project, Bucher created an app, a book with DVD (titled *100 Days of Monsters*) and KCET created

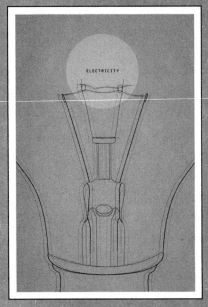

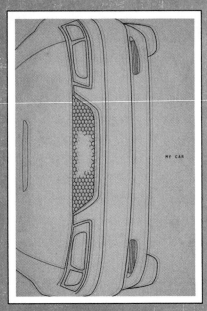

"Electricity" So many people lose electricity for days or even months (some along with their homes) because of natural disasters yet I complain when I can't use my computer due to a power outage for a couple of hours.

"My Mustang" Almost daily I still see people walking to and from work via risky roads and/or extreme weather conditions because they can't afford any other type of transportation. Yet I complained that my '99 Mustang was old and ugly.

POSTER SERIES: "The Things I Take For Granted"

DESIGNER/ILLUSTRATOR: Denyse Mitterhofer (http://mineny.com)

Denyse Mitterhofer © 2014

"In the Peru of my childhood, some kids were forced to grow up faster than they should have. You couldn't afford immaturity or naïveté. The Peru of my childhood didn't allow you that right of passage, not if you had some wealth and certainly not if you were poor.

My childhood years spent in Peru are unforgettable—the good, the bad, and the unfathomable.

I am an American citizen now, residing in the USA for over fifteen years. Here, we have every basic need answered. Not so in Peru. Although my family—of professors, attorneys and other professionals—was considered upper middle class, I recall some weeks not having electricity; the popular apagones (power blackouts) would go on for days on a monthly basis. There were nights that I had to get my homework done by candlelight—not because we couldn't afford to pay the bill but because terrorists had intentionally or unintentionally destroyed power sources.

There were times a young (sometimes a child) thief mugged my relatives for an expensive watch or a pair of trendy sneakers. We never struggled for food or clothing but we certainly appreciated it because we were surrounded by true poverty, so we knew that what we had was certainly a luxury even if we lived in a not-so-safe area.

Now I see how Peru has progressed to better and evolving districts, to shopping centers and club scenes—a very cosmopolitan life for many, at least in the major cities. So why bring back the past? Why talk about such sad times that most people bury and prefer to forget or sometimes even deny? Because there are still those countries and individuals that are struggling to get out from under. People who are still fighting terrorism, who can barely get food on their tables and sleep with an eye open at night afraid for their lives.

Yet here, we—I—complain about the most ridiculous things.

One day as I stared at my closet full of clothes, I caught myself saying: "I don't have anything to wear!" How dare I say this? (I wish I had slapped myself.) I take things for granted—from my morning coffee to the safety I enjoy in the USA. I am sometimes that complainer who always expects things to be to my liking, to accommodate me. I tell myself I am not spoiled, that I have earned each thing that I currently have but the truth is—I have taken my privilege for granted.

I have decided to celebrate the things I do have, even the silliest of things. I made a list of the things I take for granted and I turned my list into a series of posters, "The Things I Take For Granted" in the hope of reminding myself and inspiring others.

What do you take for granted?"—Denyse Mitterhofer

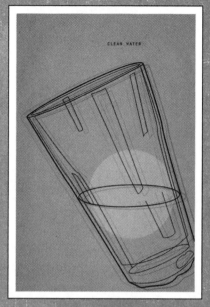

"Clean Water" There are so many countries with no clean water available. Yet, when water is the only drink available I complain it isn't good enough.

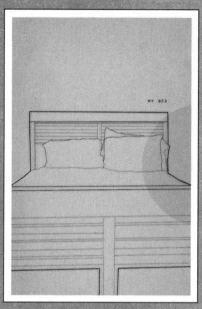

"My Bed" One night on my way back home from work, I saw a homeless man sleeping on cardboard hugging a dog. Yet I complain because I want a California bed with tons of pillows.

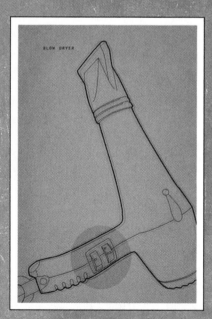

"Blow Dryer" My hair is in between curly and straight. The blow dryer helps my hair decide which one to pick for the day.

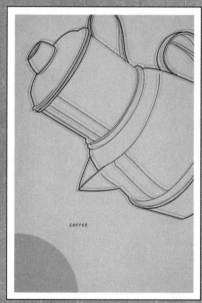

"Coffee" I went 4 days without drinking coffee because I thought I would be better off. I wasn't.

STAYING NIMBLE

ILLUSTRATION: Monster
ILLUSTRATOR: Stefan G. Bucher
©Stefan G. Bucher
(www.dailymonster.com and
www.344lovesyou.com)

an hour-long documentary on Bucher and the monsters. Bucher also created monsters for commercial clients such as Honda, and that work led to him creating the Yeti character for Saks Fifth Avenue. You can see all the monsters at www.344lovesyou.com/projects/type/monsters.

Manik Rathee, a former user experience engineer for President Barack Obama, is now a user experience engineer at Google. In his spare time, he writes about design and development and takes lots of photographs.

Designer and illustrator Jessica Hische hosts her illustrative initial cap project at Daily Drop Cap (www.dailydropcap.com). Designer Chip Kidd is in a band called ARTBREAK. Creative director and designer Allan Peters has a badge hunting series on his blog. Kai Vermehr, Steffen Sauerteig and Svend Smital of the Berlin design firm eBoy, "create re-usable pixel objects and [use] them to build complex and extensible artwork" for many clients and in their free time they build giant pixel cities, "pixelized" versions of real cities with modular isometric pieces, called Pixoramas. Each Pixorama takes two or three years to complete.

Graphic artist and illustrator Matt Lyon writes about the importance of personal work (http://mattlyonfaq.tumblr.com): "Personal work and self-initiated projects are essential for continued practice and development of skills, progression of ideas and the pursuit of personal interests." He says that his work "stems from incessant doodling, often laced with wild colors, shapes and patterns."

What's your independent project going to be?

> I try to help my students find what they are most passionate about, and how design can be used as a tool to explore those interests. Many design classes teach students how to package other people's work or brands in a pretty way. Perfect kerning and font selections can be useful, but that is not what interests me most. I want to help them learn how to think conceptually about work, and how to formulate new ideas. I want to help them understand they can use design to become authors and express themselves with these tools. I want them to feel ownership over their work and be passionate about what they are doing.
>
> —JESSICA WALSH, Partner, Sagmeister & Walsh

If Not Fearless, Then Brave

Take criticism well. When you produce creative work or work that pushes boundaries or disrupts current models, people are bound to criticize your ideas or solutions. Take it in stride and assess the criticism. Perhaps you need to dismiss it entirely. Perhaps there's something in the critical assessment that might improve what you've conceived.

As a designer or creative professional, you will have to learn to deal with it. Learn what to use and what to ignore. When asked about criticism, artist Richard Serra replied, "If the criticism is structural or intellectual in nature, and it makes sense in terms of your procedures and what you're trying to communicate, then you listen to it. If it's personal—or if it's a mixture of both—then you become very, very skeptical."

> "...I have already settled it for myself so flattery
> and criticism go down the same drain and I am quite free."
> —GEORGIA O'KEEFFE

CHAPTER 06

INTERVIEWS

MARK AVNET

DEAN OF 360iU

As dean of 360i's educational center, 360iU, Mark is charged with educating employees on cross-functional skills to inspire big ideas catalyzed by the collaboration of strategy, technology and creative. For 360i's roster of Fortune 500 marketers, Mark advises on how to leverage digital technologies to create closer connections between people and brands.

Mark has more than twenty-five years of experience in media, technology and education. Prior to 360i, he was a professor and chair of the Creative Technology Track at the Virginia Commonwealth University (VCU) Brandcenter, widely heralded as the nation's top graduate school in advertising and marketing.

Avnet's agency background includes time at Ammirati Purls Lintas's APL Digital as SVP and Director of Production & Technology, and time at Lot21 Interactive Marketing as CTO and head of its Emerging Media Development Lab.

Photo courtesy of 360i

Mark holds a Master's Degree in Interactive Telecommunications from New York University and a Master's Degree in Media Psychology from Fielding Graduate University.

How does your agency foster a culture of ideas, experimentation and collaboration?

We have built 360i to be powered by curiosity. For us, that means constantly asking *Why?* and looking for those sometimes hidden threads that connect different ideas, thoughts, insights, feelings and behaviors, and then creating from that something new that achieves our clients' goals. Rather than focusing on what we know, we focus on what we don't know about consumer behavior and how it is rapidly evolving, especially when it comes to how people are using mobile, social and technology. We want to identify all the ways brands can engage in authentic and relevant ways.

Because we grew from a digital start-up, unencumbered by the way traditional agencies are run—based on silos and separate departments—our process has been collaborative from the start. In fact, it almost has to be for us to do the digital-centric work we do, and to build marketing strategies for a rapidly changing technological ecosystem that intersects with a rapidly changing culture.

This is not to say we're about the technology—we rarely start with tech in our thinking. We start with our clients' goals, what their audience needs, the currency that will drive those connections that give these brands the authority to speak to those audiences in a mutually beneficial manner, and finally what will be the best way to connect the dots. And often the best way has a digital, social or technological component.

To come up with better ideas, we make sure that our meetings include a mix of subject matter experts who represent cross-discipline expertise, as early as possible. Some agencies talk about T-shaped thinkers; I like to think of ours as being Tetris-shaped—not just a single deep descender, but the ability to think deeply across a number of areas, to fit dynamically into the changing landscape in which we work.

We value curiosity and experimentation. It's how humans (and agencies) learn and develop. So experimentation is a deeply engrained part of our culture—everything from prototyping in the lab, to thought experiments, to running pilot test-and-learns with clients and vendors. We value learning and iteration, taking the results of our marketing engagements and experiments and applying the lessons to enhance our performance the next time around.

In addition to focusing on earning the rewards of good client relationships and industry recognition, we reward good ideas internally by making sure they're heard in the first place and that the people who have them get credit for them, even when the idea evolves to something different. We make sure that the provenance is clear.

How do you educate employees on cross-functional skills to inspire big ideas?

Training has always been a priority at 360i, and we launched 360iU three years ago to bring more academic rigor to our educational and professional development programs, helping ensure support for a diverse community of thinkers. My background is in both advertising and education, and as dean of 360iU, I ensure our programs have useful outcomes and that they are designed to help us think across channels, across disciplines and across domains. We have courses in different ideation techniques, presentation skills, creative technology, journalism, even how to manage and prioritize everyday workflow in order to clear up time to think. Our classes and workshops are open to everyone at the agency, and we are constantly working to ensure we have a good mix of departments represented. When someone has something they'd like to teach, I'll work with them to develop a good program and find an opportunity for them to present either as a stand-alone class or as part of one of our ongoing series of drop-in sessions.

How does your agency create authentic experiences?

Our ability to do this ties back to consumer behavior and understanding how consumer behavior can help us reimagine the role of a brand in consumers' lives. Because people's behavior is rapidly evolving, we are in constant pursuit of knowing how people discover brands and share stories, and this helps us create campaigns that connect with consumers in relevant and authentic ways.

How do you leverage digital technologies to create closer connections between people and brands?

We strive to be the best digital-centric communications agency with integrated earned, owned and paid capabilities. That is, we look for the best strategy, based on insights about a brand and people, that solves our clients' business challenges, and then look for the best mediating platform or technology to bring everyone together. Sometimes that's television or print or radio or OOH, but often there's a digital touch point or insight that may be closer to the life people are living—especially as the world gets more mobile and social, and people increasingly use digital devices to connect. So we make sure that we acknowledge how people are living, and then build the connections based on that—by keeping our thinking "digital/social/mobile by design" and not making digital an add-on. We're not tied to a single favorite platform, or even two or three. By having a very deep knowledge of all the platforms people use, from traditional to the latest digital and technology innovations, we can design our programs to work across all the platforms in ways that make the most sense for each program.

How do you help people become creative makers?

What's the old adage—give someone a fish, they eat for a day, but teach them to fish and they can eat for a lifetime? We help people learn to fish. We do this by encouraging big thinking and by answering the question "Is it possible to...?" with a resounding "Yes!"

But more importantly, we get people over the paralyzing fear of making mistakes that can stop them from even trying. Getting hands-on with tools and tech, showing how easy it is to use things like IFTTT or a MakerBot, helping people ease into Arduino through Lego Mindstorms, or putting ad hoc teams together for a pet project—all of these things inspire and help people realize that they can think of things outside their area of expertise and make stuff that actually works.

Our lab, open to everyone, is stocked with all sorts of tools and toys, and anyone who wants to learn how to do something is able to. For people who aren't ready to be hands-on, they can submit an idea and we'll figure out how to bring it to life. In that way, ideation becomes an important part of being a creative maker.

What kind of mind-set is optimal for digital marketing?

Really easy: Start with people. Always start with people. What do they need? What are they trying to do in their lives? Then look at the brand: What does it have to offer that might help people do whatever they're trying to do? Does it have the cultural authority to offer that to a particular audience? If so, what creative things can we do, knowing what's possible from a technological standpoint, that will connect people and the brand? And then we can apply all the great stuff we know from advertising and marketing experience to build on the things that work. It's important to learn from everyone's history, not just from a postmortem of our own work.

Long and short: Starting with technology might make you a great production company, but starting with people can help you become a great strategic and creative marketer.

What is a creative technology mind-set?

I came up with this when I founded and ran the creative technology track at VCU Brandcenter and have adopted it as 360iU's motto: learn, do, teach.

It's important to learn, and then you have to apply what you've learned. To really make it part of yourself, you have to teach it as well. But teaching isn't mono-directional. When you teach something, you clarify what it means, and you also open yourself up to learning how what you're teaching can apply to someone else—that's cross-pollination coming into the forefront.

Since the goal of creative technology is to be strategic and creative in a technologically mediated world, a creative technology mind-set also means being hungry to keep a few steps ahead. One of my favorite questions about technology is what else can it do? We need to always be looking for new ways to connect things and people. Culture and technology change all the time, so our thinking about them can't be static.

Interview © 360i, 2014.

LIZ BLAZER

FILMMAKER AND ANIMATOR (WWW.LIZBLAZER.COM)

Liz Blazer is a filmmaker, art director, visual artist, designer, animator and educator. She has worked as a development artist for Disney, a special effects designer for MTV, and as an art director for the Palestinian/Israeli *Sesame Street*. Her animated documentary *Backseat Bingo* traveled to 180 film festivals in 15 countries and won many awards, including awards from the HBO Comedy Arts Festival, *Animation Magazine* and the International Documentary Association. One of her favorite projects was creating and directing *Food Court Diaries*, a series of animated documentary shorts for the Cartoon Network. Blazer enjoys the challenge of teaching. She is a high-energy professor who emphasizes storytelling and pitching as she guides her students to bring their designs to life through animation. Peachpit will publish Blazer's new book, *Motion Graphic Storytelling*.

PHOTO CREDIT: Anna Herbst, Orange Studios

What skills does an effective animator need?

An effective animator needs a firm grasp on the fundamentals of design (a good sense of color, form, type and composition). But what separates good animation from great is timing. Great animators have a natural sense of rhythm and movement, which allows them to guide their audience's attention. Timing controls the emotional flow of a piece and can help set tone and build story. Some of the best animators I know are experienced in other art forms where timing is critical. Musicians, dancers and oral storytellers are adept at using rhythms expressively, utilizing pauses to create tension, and shifting tempo to build to a climax. Animators need to be as intentional about timing as they are with character design, story and dialogue.

What makes for a compelling animation?

Structure. Whether your piece is a fairy tale with an obvious beginning, middle and end, or an abstract music-and-color piece featuring blue squares that turn into red circles, compelling animation requires clear structure. A strong structure begins in preproduction with storyboards. There's a misconception that great art should be created in a frenzy of creativity. The first thing I do with my students is set aside that romantic notion. Building an animated piece requires as much forethought and preparation as building a house. You don't just start throwing bricks on top of each other no matter what the Muse tells you, so don't build your animated world that way. Map out your whole piece before you start working on selected scenes. Your planning will manifest itself as intention. Once your piece is complete, your audience will be far more willing to go along for the ride.

What makes for a compelling story in animation?

A great animated story exploits the limitless possibilities of the medium.
    Story requires a strong plot, human themes, interesting conflict, relatable characters, and a sense of a new journey. But a strong animated story is playful with the elasticity of the visual form. Animation can be magic, so once you know what it is you are trying to say, utilize the many visual ways it can be expressed.

What is the best advice you have ever given or received about animation and storytelling?

Two pieces of advice stick out, both exercises in discipline:

1. Force yourself to create a tag, a logline and an elevator pitch for your piece. Think of a tag as an enticing slogan, like "Don't Go in the Water" for the film *Jaws*. A logline is a one-sentence summary of your project and conveys what the story is about, including what conflict is being presented in the most abbreviated way possible. An elevator pitch is a way to quickly sell your project to someone who knows nothing about it. If you can't tell someone the essence of your story in the span of a quick elevator ride, then you probably don't know what it is.

2. Make a production timeline and stick to it. The trick is to set small achievable goals, then check them off as you go. Skills and confidence will build with each small accomplishment.

How do you create the pace of the story or the moment the audience is waiting for in an animation?

It takes work. I use storyboards, mind maps and animatics to analyze the beats of my piece. An animatic is made from inserting the rough storyboard sketches into a video timeline with sound. Animatics are instrumental in previsualizing the flow of the piece. Once I understand the beats of the story I lay out the dialogue, music and sound effects to get a feel for pacing and experiment with timing the shots. Pacing is one of the hardest things to learn and is a skill that generally comes from trial and error. I'm a firm believer in preproduction—it is like having a great map when you leave on a road trip.

Pacing story in animation is all about choosing when to reveal information. It's a good idea to hook your audience early with a question then follow it up with small bits of new information. Audiences love to do detective work. Allow them to participate in the journey of your film by laying a breadcrumb trail that leads to your conclusion.

You create imagined worlds. How do you set up the rules of your constructed worlds?

First, an animator must learn and respect the laws of the natural world. I encourage my students to observe nature with an eye on the basic laws of physics. Observe an animal running, a fork falling from a table, a light bulb swaying. Note gravity's pull on that object. Once the animator understands and respects the effect of gravity on weight, it is up to him or her to turn those rules on their head to tell his or her story. A teacup falling from a table will fall at a similar rate on different days due to the laws of physics; however, an invaluable heirloom teacup that falls from a table while a horrified auctioneer looks on will slow down and speed up to maximize emotional impact. Once an animator establishes all the rules in his or her world, I encourage trying a test. Say in your world liquids turn to solids when exposed to light. What happens when it rains? Can people drink after dawn? I recommend that animators who are creating their own worlds throw themselves multiple curve balls to test the laws of their own creation.

The hardest part for many aspiring visual communicators is coming up with a viable idea. What sparks ideas for your work? Take us through your ideation or design process.

My ideation process is one of long-term collecting and collage. I accumulate things that interest and inspire me. I keep well-organized folders of character designs, background designs, color palettes, textures, trees, shapes and short animated pieces that I love. This helps me define my taste and gives me preapproved jumping off points, so I'm ready to react to new projects from many design angles. I am also always seeking new influences, heroes and friends whose work I follow and am inspired by. Social media is an amazing way to become friends with and keep an eye on your chosen tastemakers. Over time I have so many inspirations I have bookmarked that there are multiple projects I would like to do. Time is the problem, not lack of ideas!

Animation is constantly growing as a medium. If you were to teach a workshop in animation or motion, what would you stress?

- Storytelling: Technology changes, but humanity has been telling the same kinds of stories for thousands of years. It is a skill that matters and can be improved upon with steady work.
- Technical skills: These need to be developed alongside storytelling and critical thinking skills. Students often figure out what they want to make as they experiment with the technical side of the medium.
- The Start Now Principle: Growth comes with practice, so students should begin making short films right away no matter what level they are at. With practice and patience students will find their voice and their own message inside the medium.

INTERVIEW WITH

DR. PETER GRAY

RESEARCH PROFESSOR, PSYCHOLOGY, BOSTON COLLEGE

Peter Gray, Ph.D., has conducted and published research in neuroendo-crinology, developmental psychology, anthropology and education. He is author of an internationally acclaimed introductory psychology text-book (*Psychology*, Worth Publishers, now in its 6th edition), which views all of psychology from an evolutionary perspective. His recent research focuses on the role of play in human evolution and how children educate themselves through play and exploration when they are free to do so. He has expanded on these ideas in his recent book, *Free to Learn: Why Unleashing the Instinct to Play Will Make Our Children Happier, More Self-Reliant, and Better Students for Life* (Basic Books, 2013). He also authors a regular blog called *Freedom to Learn*, for *Psychology Today* magazine. His own current play life includes not only his research and writing, but also long-distance bicycling, backwoods skiing, pond skating, kayaking, and backyard vegetable gardening.

What is the connection between play and creativity?

Play, by definition, is creative activity; it always involves an element of imagination. Play always has structure, but within that structure there is always room for creativity, and that is part of what makes the activity play. Many research studies have shown that people think more creatively and produce more creative products when they are in a playful mood than when they are in a more serious mood. Highly creative people regularly refer to their activities as play. Einstein, for example, referred to his accomplishments in theoretical physics and mathematics as "combinatory play." He developed his theory of relativity in part by imagining himself chasing a sunbeam and catching up to it. Geniuses seem to be those people who retain into adulthood the childlike capacity for play.

What are the most important skills learned through play?

My research into the lives of hunter-gatherer children convinces me that children are biologically designed to play in ways that promote the full range of human skills. Children play at physical skills, linguistic skills, skills of manual construction, intellectual skills, social skills and emotional skills. I also see all this at the Sudbury Valley School, where children and adolescents control their own education and are free to play and explore in their own chosen ways essentially all day long, every day, and educate themselves in this way. In *Free to Learn*, I describe how play provides the foundation for all of these aspects of human development.

What is the lifelong value of play?

The most direct way of answering this is to say that play is what makes life worthwhile. A life without play would be dreary indeed. Play, by definition, is what we want to do as opposed to what we feel compelled to do. Adult "work" is playful to the degree that adults enjoy it. Sociologists studying employment satisfaction have found that the qualities of a job that lead to the most satisfaction are those qualities that make the work playful: autonomy (freedom to choose how and when to do the work, no micromanagement by bosses), creativity (the work could not be done by a robot), and challenge (play is never easy, because when it is easy it becomes boring and is no longer play).

Why is it important to not fear failure?

Any new venture involves risk of failure. Fear of failure prevents innovation. The playful state of mind does not fear failure. Failure is how we learn.

Why is creativity a key to economic success?

Creativity is a key to economic success now even more so than in the past. We have machines to do most of the noncreative activities: robots to assemble things, computers to do routine calculations, search engines to find answers to already-answered questions. Economic success for individuals today requires the ability to do things that machines can't do, and those things essentially always involve creativity.

What is the evolutionary purpose of curiosity?

Curiosity is the drive to explore and learn about the environment, including the social environment as well as the physical environment. All mammals are curious, because all mammals need to explore and learn about their environment—to find water, food, mates, dangers, shelters and the other necessities of life and reproduction. We humans have the most to learn and therefore natural selection has shaped us to be the most curious of all animals. Within hours of their birth, infants are already exploring their environment with their eyes; for example, they look toward novel patterns more than toward patterns they have already seen. Within months they are exploring any objects that they can reach with their hands, and when they become mobile they are attracted to all that is new and want to manipulate those objects to understand their properties. As children get still older, they explore with language. They ask questions, listen to people talk, and in that way learn about things that are not right in front of them. Human beings are especially curious about other human beings and their activities. Children throughout the world learn by observing their elders carefully (not just adults, but even more so, older children) and incorporating their activities into their own play. Curiosity, playfulness and sociability are the fundamental human characteristics that make us the cultural animal. This is how culture is acquired and built upon by each new generation of human beings. I describe these as our educative instincts, because education, broadly defined, is cultural acquisition.

What inhibits creative thinking?

The primary inhibitor of creative thinking is fear. A somewhat oversimplified but nevertheless useful way to look at this question is as follows: When real danger is present, we are biologically programmed to use our already-learned ways of dealing with that danger. Our creative mind shuts down and we go into a high adrenaline mode of using great energy to do what is already second nature to us. When a real tiger is present, that is not the time to try out new, creative ways of dealing with a tiger. We are biologically designed to try out new ways of thinking and behaving when there is no real danger present—for example, when we are pretending to escape from an imaginary tiger (in the guise of a playmate) in our play. In our culture, fear of others' judgments and fear of failure (which is usually related to others' judgments) are the biggest inhibitors of creativity. The playful state of mind is one in which such fears are set aside.

In creative activities and play, is the means more valuable than the ends at times?

One of the defining characteristics of full-fledged play is that the means are valued more than the ends. Even where there are clear ends, it is the achievement of the ends, not the ends themselves, that are valued. Children build a sandcastle not so they can have a sandcastle (it will be washed into the sea with the next tide anyway), but to enjoy the process of building it: building it to their own specifications, building it beautiful. In competitive games that are truly play, children and adults enjoy the process of scoring points and winning, but if it is truly play, they soon forget who won or lost because there are no real-world consequences for it. This is one of the reasons why pick-up sports are play while adult-organized sports for children are not. The focus on means is part of what makes play such a powerful method of education. In play, one can experiment with new ways of doing things without fear of failure, because failure in play has no serious consequences for your survival or well-being.

INTERVIEW WITH

DAVE GLASS & KILL COOPER

DAVE GLASS, ARTIST AND FOUNDER OF HUNGRY CASTLE

AND KILL COOPER, ARTIST, HUNGRY CASTLE

Based in Barcelona, Hungry Castle is a creative studio that specializes in creating public art and fashion, which they call Cool Shit. Working collectively since 2011 the goal has always been to make big, playful things of cultural impact and use design thinking in a way that truly engages people. Influenced by Shepard Fairey's prolific use of public space, the artists combine unique 3-D pieces with large-scale production à la Jeff Koons, but Hungry Castle adds an interactive ingredient to create a fully immersive experience between audience and art.

Hungry Castle sells concepts and Cool Shit to a cross section of clients and sponsors including Adidas, HP and several International Music Festivals. Their work has been exhibited in New York, the U.K., Spain and Miami Beach.

Artist and founder of Hungry Castle, Dave Glass (aka Danger) was born in Australia. He completed his studies at The College of Fine Arts Sydney and has a decades' worth of advertising agency experience. He is known for combining public art and fashion with his unique creative vision. He loves the strange, the beautiful and creating larger-than-life projects.

Kill Cooper (aka the Killa from Manila, although he's Irish) has a degree in visual communications and other studio notches on his belt. Kill is an artist who believes that one of the greatest things in life is coming up with ideas and realizing them. He likes to think big, very big—big ideas with a twist of crazy and a generous slice of humor.

Why did you form your studio—and why did you name it Hungry Castle?

> **DANGER:** We formed Hungry Castle because we got restless with doing boring shit for other people.
>
> **KILL:** We liked the sound of [the name] and the image these words paint in people's imaginations.

What are your studio's guiding principles?

> **DANGER:** We have a very simple manifesto.
>
> 1. Make it bigger.
> 2. Keep it simple.
> 3. Have fun.

You've said the Internet is your muse. Why is that? How do you use it to spark ideas for your work?

> **DANGER:** Life is a big inspiration for our work, the Internet just happens to be where all the freaky shit ends up (depending on where you look of course). We love the Internet because it connects people with ideas. Everyone is an artist online. Anyone can start a meme or create something that is appreciated by millions. We take ideas that are already out there and make them our own.
>
> In the case of [our project] "Laser Cat" some bored cat owner out there in la-la land took a photo of his feline friend, the eyes reflected with the flash of his camera, and he coined the term "Laser Cat" for the caption. People have been paying tribute to the Laser Cat meme

**GIANT INFLATABLE SCULP-
TURE:** "Lionel Ritchie's Head"
by Hungry Castle
HUNGRY CASTLE © 2014
PHOTO CREDIT: © Jean-Marc
Joseph (jm-joseph.com)

LARGE-SCALE SCULPTURE:
"Big Bird" by Hungry Castle
HUNGRY CASTLE © 2014
Photo credit: © Jean-Marc
Joseph (jm-joseph.com)

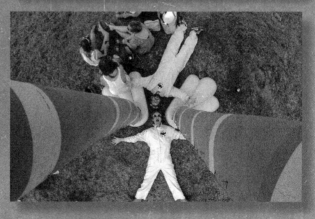

LARGE-SCALE SCULPTURE:
"Big Bird" by Hungry Castle
HUNGRY CASTLE © 2014
Photo credit: © Jean-Marc
Joseph (jm-joseph.com)

since. We just made it bigger, added real lasers and decided to tour the world with it.

Please tell us about your creative process.

DANGER: There is no guaranteed creative process. Sometimes we start with a problem that needs to be solved. Other times we start with a solution that actually requires a problem. That might sound like some artsy-fartsy crap right there, but it's true.

With our sculpture titled "Lionel Richie's Head" it was clear for a long time that we wanted to build the giant noggin. The challenge was trying to explain why and persuade the lovely community of Kickstarter to part with £8,016 to help us do it.

What is the best advice you've received about your work?

KILL: A year into Hungry Castle, an acclaimed art director said he thought our best work was personal. The world was responding more to our personal projects compared to the commercial stuff. His words gave us the courage to take more risks, to do what we loved and to create Cool Shit we are passionate about.

How do you set up the rules of your constructed worlds?

KILL: The Cool Shit we make always has to be playful, public, prodigious and pop.

How do you create work that people want to engage with? How do you structure a piece to get people to participate?

DANGER: In 2006 Time magazine chose "You" for Person of the Year. It was a tribute to the millions of people who anonymously contribute to content online (on Wikipedia, YouTube, etc.). This always resonated with me, but for a different reason. We believe that to make something truly engaging, whether it is an artwork or an iPhone app, it has to be about "you."

We spend weeks, months and sometimes years trying to focus on that single interaction. That single moment that will strike a dialogue between the piece and "you." Sometimes we get lucky and we nail it and sometimes we don't. Regardless of the outcome, we love "you" and we think "you" are the most important element of our work.

If you were to teach a workshop in creativity or innovation, what would you emphasize?

DANGER: Mario Andretti once said, "If everything seems under control, you're not going fast enough." My version would be, "If everything you do is accepted, then you're not pushing your ideas hard enough." Try not to seek acceptance, forge your own path and make your own mistakes. But most importantly make sure you do something. Talking about it doesn't count. Get out there and make it happen.

INTERVIEW WITH

REI INAMOTO

CHIEF CREATIVE OFFICER, AKQA

Rei Inamoto is one of the most influential individuals in the marketing and creative industry today. He was named in *Creativity* magazine's annual "Creativity 50" as well as one of the "Top 25 Most Creative People in Advertising" in *Forbes Magazine*.

With broad international experience in Asia, Europe and the U.S. as well as an unusual combination of background in advertising, design and technology, Rei brings a unique perspective to his work.

Rei is chief creative officer of AKQA, responsible for delivering creative solutions for the agency's clients such as Audi, Google, Nike and Xbox. Since he arrived at the agency in 2005, his presence has been instrumental in bringing AKQA the highest recognitions. In 2009, AKQA became the first agency in history to receive five Agency of the Year accolades from publications such as *Creative Review* and *Campaign*. It was also selected as one of the *Fast Company*'s "50 Most Innovative Companies" as well as recognized by *Advertising Age* as one of the ten "Agencies of the Decade." In

2012, Rei was inducted into "The Hall of Achievement" by the American Advertising Federation, honoring the top young talent of the industry.

Rei is a frequent speaker at numerous conferences such as Cannes Lions International Festival of Creativity, SXSW and Spikes Asia, to name a few. His writing and opinions have been widely published in publications like *Fast Company* and *Contagious* magazine, making him a thought leader and a prominent voice in the industry.

Originally from Tokyo, Rei spent his childhood and teenage years in Japan and Europe. He then went to the U.S. to complete his university studies with degrees in fine arts and computer science—all before people were broadcasting their feelings, talking in 140 characters or fewer, or becoming friends with people they didn't know.

He currently resides in New York.

What are your agency's guiding principles?
Innovation. Service. Quality. Thought.

Advertising has shifted from making artifacts to creating content that engages and benefits people. What strategies can you offer creative professionals for working in this new era?
Be clear about the consumer problem you are trying to solve. Don't try to solve too many problems at once, because you'll end up solving none. [Don't focus on] problems just from a brand's point of view, because most people may not care.

You have said, "Creativity and innovation are about finding unexpected solutions to obvious problems or finding obvious solutions to unexpected problems." What guidance can you offer to creative professionals on how to best prepare for those challenges?
FIRST, choose a craft and really learn it.
SECOND, start making your ideas. Without making them, they are no good.
THIRD, simplify. It can always be simpler.

Nike+ Kinect Training Exercise Game
AGENCY: AKQA
CLIENT: Nike+ Kinect Training

From AKQA: "Nike+ Kinect Training redefines personal fitness at home, offering the same training techniques provided to elite Nike athletes. From revolutionary footwear to digital products and services, Nike has from day one empowered athletes to reach their full potential. Today, the best way to get fit and stay fit is with a personal trainer. By combining Nike's experience in athletic training with Xbox Kinect's powerful full body sensor technology, for the first time, we can now give everyone a motivating and effective personal trainer in their home."

How have you adapted to rapid changes in the profession during the span of your career?

Jean-Baptiste Alphonse Karr said, "The more things change, the more they stay the same."

What skills and characteristics allow creative professionals to move up the ladder?

First, work hard and be good to people.
Second, work needs to speak for itself.
Third, have and show integrity.

How do you fabricate brand stories or construct contexts for content that engages people? How do you create work that people will want to share?

It goes back to the early question about content (or utility) that engages and benefits people. The most important step to problem solving is finding the right problem to solve. The problem with most problems is not reframing the problem in the first place.

How do you create work that steps outside of the norm?

Keep asking: Is this something that was possible five years ago?

What is the most important lesson you have learned in your career?

Paul Arden said, "It's not how good you are, it's how good you want to be."

DR. MIZUKO ITO

CULTURAL ANTHROPOLOGIST AT UNIVERSITY OF CALIFORNIA, IRVINE

(WWW.ITOFISHER.COM/MITO)

Mizuko Ito is a cultural anthropologist of technology use, examining children and youth's changing relationships to media and communications. She is Research Director of the Digital Media and Learning Hub, University of California Humanities Research Institute and also Professor in Residence and John D. and Catherine T. MacArthur Foundation Chair in Digital Media and Learning, Department of Anthropology and Department of Informatics and School of Education, University of California, Irvine. Her work on educational software appears in *Engineering Play: A Cultural History of Children's Software.* In Japan, her research has focused on mobile and portable technologies; her findings are presented in *Personal, Portable, Pedestrian: Mobile Phones in Japanese Life,* which she edited with Daisuke Okabe and Misa Matsuda. She has led a three-year collaborative ethnographic study, funded by the MacArthur Foundation, examining youth new media practices in the U.S., and focusing on gaming, digital media production, and Internet use. The findings of this project are reported in *Hanging Out, Messing Around, and Geeking Out: Youth Living and Learning with New Media.*

Her book on anime fandom *Fandom Unbound: Otaku Culture in a Connected World* was released in 2012 from Yale University Press. The *Connected Learning* report that was released by her team in January, 2013 is available online (http://dmlhub.net/publications/connected-learning-agenda-research-and-design).

How can people use "messing around" or "geeking out" on the online world to learn? How does it foster creativity, intellectual engagement or civic engagement?

Experimentation, exploration and social exchange have always been central to meaningful learning. Today's online world, which includes rich content as well as social media, offers an abundance of opportunity for exploratory and social learning. Learners can look around, "mess around," experiment and lurk with very low costs and low barriers to entry. Finding out about a new interest or seeking an answer to a thorny problem can be as simple as Googling, finding a YouTube video, or lurking on an expert forum. FAQs, tutorials, how-to videos, and detailed answers on Q&A forums litter the Internet, created by experts, enthusiasts and hobbyists of all shapes and sizes. And for someone who is going deep into a specialty area of interest, the Internet is a way to easily connect with others who share these interests and expertise and to "geek out." Online tools to geek out are getting more and more sophisticated with the development of new kinds of educational offerings, online community norms, reputation systems, and ways of sharing and curating content. It can be difficult to find one's way and to cull through the less worthy content, but for the committed enthusiast the online world offers a treasure trove for geeking out.

Unlike more formal and sequential learning, this kind of exploratory, informal and social learning is driven by the needs and interests of the learner and is more engaging and personally meaningful than most classroom education. Because it is tied to authentic curiosity and inquiry, the learner is in a position of being creative and productive rather than simply absorbing a proscribed curriculum where the answers are already known in advance. The social context for geeked-out communities also provides many opportunities for participants to contribute to the authentic life of a community, whether that is through community organizing, moderating or providing content. These kinds of experiences of contributing to communities are an important dimension of civic engagement and can be a gateway to other forms of civic and political action even outside the specific interest area.

How can anthropology inspire new designs? What role can an anthropologist play on a design or creative team?

Over the years I've participated in many design and technology development teams, taking different kinds of roles. Anthropologists can play a role in all phases of design and development. When I first started out, in graduate school, I worked at places like Apple and Xerox PARC observing how software that was already developed was taken up by users in real-life settings and feeding that back into the improvement of the technology. Often this was about pointing out failures and misunderstandings due to the social and cultural distance between the designers and users. I've also done more exploratory work, where we are looking at a particular site of practice, like television viewing or photo sharing, considering the kinds of needs that new technology might fill.

I think my favorite role is one that I'm taking right now in my work on connected learning, which is to observe and engage with communities that exemplify what we think are positive social and cultural dynamics, and then to learn from these existing practices what kinds of tools, technologies and techniques might be spread. I've been inspired by the "positive deviance" approach, which is a way of elevating the positive practices that already exist in communities and spreading them to other communities facing similar problems. The positive deviance movement, which originated in public health, has some similarities with participatory design approaches that have been around in the technology sector for a while, but there is a stronger emphasis on finding solutions that already exist among the communities in question. Whether it is positive deviance or participatory design, these approaches differ fundamentally from a more common approach to technology-driven change, where the designers and developers come up with expert solutions on their own that they try to disseminate or scale to communities with a perceived problem or lack. Often these more top-down approaches fail because designers don't have awareness of the contexts that their target communities operate in or because of lack of buy-in and ownership in these user communities.

With connected learning, this approach has meant seeking out youth, parents, communities and educators leveraging new technology for progressive education, and elevating their practices in ways that enable others to identify with them and take them up. Often anthropology has focused on social problems and technology failures, which is an important message for designers and technology makers. I also think, however, that anthropology's stance of careful listening, observation and attentiveness to social and cultural context is a natural fit with positive deviance approaches. I feel it is important for social scientists to be critical and point out social ills, as well as provide positive inspiration for design and social change.

What is the role of design in your research?

There are two ways I engage with design in my research. One is through the observation of existing communities and practices, I identify the often implicit design principles and features of the environment that have grown up organically. For example, in high-functioning connected learning environments, we've found that there are certain shared design features, such as the ability to give thoughtful peer-to-peer feedback, reputation systems that reward high quality work, and social rewards for helping others. These design principles and features in turn can become a source of guidance and inspiration for others who are seeking to design for and support connected learning.

The other way I engage in design is by being part of an interdisciplinary team that is designing and deploying something in the world. Developing online tools and technologies is an ideal kind of setting for an anthropologist to participate in, because it is about constant iterative development in real-life contexts with real users. Right now I am part of a team developing a new set of learning opportunities online that are inspired by our research on online interest communities and digital youth, and I get to work with a team that includes software developers, community managers and product managers on a constantly evolving set of online offerings.

How does appropriation (common in fan or remix culture) enhance or limit creativity?

Often people think of creativity as born from solitary inspiration, but I think for many if not most people creativity happens in the context of working with found materials and in the context of social exchange and communication. I've loved remix culture and fan culture because it is a very accessible form of creative practice that bridges between everyday media consumption and professional media production. Whether it is fan fiction, fan art or remix videos, these forms of cultural production are about making something new and creative as part of an ongoing conversation with other fans and media producers. It recognizes that creativity always builds on the prior work of others, and it celebrates this fact. It can also be a stepping stone to forms of creative production that are more "original" because fan creators are developing the literacy and skills of media production that are at the heart of any kind of media creation.

How does new media inspire imagination in everyday life?

When I was doing research over a decade ago on the first generation of camera phones that were spreading in Tokyo, I was amazed at how the presence of an always-available digital camera changes people's perception of their physical environment. Early camera phone users talked about a kind of heightened visual awareness because there was always an opportunity to capture a photo, and they were taking pictures that were much more creative and artistic than the standard kinds of snapshots that historically dominated amateur photography. The photo might be of a pretty pastry, but it could also be of a striking view from an escalator that someone rides every day on his or her way to work. We saw very few examples of the posed group snapshots or travel photos that were more common fare for amateur photos. I used to take photos of the bento boxes I packed for my kids every morning when they were little, and I loved that stream of little but pretty everyday ephemera. Now, in the era of Instagram and Snapchat this kind of pervasive, ongoing image capture is now an unremarkable aspect of everyday life and communication, but it's important to remember that this sensibility is relatively new and was developed hand in hand with new media capture and production tools.

The advent of low cost digital cameras of all shapes and sizes and of free and cheap digital production tools has led to an explosion of amateur media creation in the past decade. We can now look for inspiration not only to professional creators or immediate neighbors and peers, but to a whole host of everyday, amateur, as well as professional creators that are sharing their work through the global web. This means that we are much more likely to find work that speaks to and inspires us, as well as that we can much more easily connect to the audiences that most want to hear from us, whether that is a grandmother who wants to hear my daughter's viola recital or a graduate student who is really interested in ethnographic methods. This ability to easily capture, produce and share media, as well as connect with other creators and audiences continues to inspire storytelling, media creation and the imagination in everyday life.

You've collaborated with experts from different disciplines. How does collaboration foster creativity?

I find collaborating with experts in other disciplines both inspiring and humbling. It is an important reminder of the unique expertise and value that I bring to collaboration as well as a reminder of how little I actually know beyond my specialty. My favorite collaborations involve working with people with very different forms of expertise but where we share common goals and values. These are also the kinds of collaborations that spark creativity because we happen on unexpected points of intersection, conflict and synergy that produce more innovative outcomes. For example, I currently help lead a MacArthur Foundation research network on Connected Learning that includes designers, psychologists, sociologists and an economist. We all share a commitment to a vision of social change and educational reform that benefits all young people, but we approach this issue through very different lenses and methodologies. By bringing together mixed methods research and varied approaches to design and practice, I like to think that we are coming up with more creative solutions than if we represented a more narrow range of specialties.

SARAH NELSON JACKSON

PARTNER & CREATIVE DIRECTOR, WESHOULDDOITALL (WSDIA)

Sarah Nelson Jackson is principal of WeShouldDoItAll (WSDIA), a contemporary design studio that translates clients' needs into dynamic, visual systems that can be presented at multiple scales. These solutions take the form of branding, interactive, books, environmental or spatial projects. Sarah is from New Jersey, where she immersed herself in fine arts and art history, later discovering her admiration for graphic design.

Sarah has a multifaceted design portfolio, which includes a rebrand and design system overhaul for ESPN International Marketing Solutions and packaging of an exclusive limited edition case housing Nike's latest elite training gear products for NFL athletes. Under the umbrella of Ralph Appelbaum Associates, WSDIA is one of the lead exhibition design teams for the David Adjaye designed Smithsonian National Museum of African American History and Culture (NMAAHC). Past clients include American Institute of Architects New York (AIA NY) Center for Architecture; the Institute for Urban Design; Art Directors Club of New York (ADC);

Columbia University Graduate School of Architecture, Planning and Preservation (GSAPP); University of Pennsylvania School of Design; Diesel; *The New York Times Magazine*; and the Trust for Governors Island.

Sarah has lectured at the Art Directors Club, the Apple Store Soho, the University of Michigan Taubman College of Architecture and Urban Planning, and for AIGA/NY.

Sarah graduated from Boston University with a B.F.A. in Graphic Design and a minor in Art History. She previously worked for graphic design offices Ingredient, AREA 17 and Helicopter.

What is your studio's guiding principle?

Designers, and all other professionals, should not feel constrained to some singular expertise. To survive our own creative game, it is imperative to know that there is not one absolute solution to any given problem. Immersing oneself in different avenues of creativity forces consideration of the otherwise unconsidered. It's that method of working that's exciting and motivating for the studio's practice.

How do you establish a creative atmosphere in your studio that allows original work to emerge? Why do you take dance breaks during work?

We strive to maintain an atmosphere that is not overly structured—that encourages discovery, play and individual and collaborative exploration. To put it simply, we keep things relatively light and open. Our process focuses a lot on research and historical reference, but we also spend a lot of time word mapping, sketching and creating quick models that allow original ideas to come to life. We encourage trial and error: make mistakes, start over—the process is just as (or more) fulfilling as the result.

We also think a lot about slowing down, about the centering and mindfulness that comes from turning off your Twitter-Instagram-Facebook-email-RSS-feeds and reading a book, handwriting a letter, building a model or sketching with a pencil. There's an incredible reward we find from these mediums that inspires us and helps to inform our space and work.

We take dance breaks to keep the blood flowing! While what we do is important and ultimately can solve problems and affect culture and society, dance breaks encourage us not to take ourselves too seriously. It's also a reminder that sometimes work can and should be fun. We simply like to dance!

When you work for clients, how do you avoid creative constraints?
People may not admit it, but to an extent we like rules, direction and instruction. We actually thrive when given creative constraints; it gives us a clear problem to solve and foundational elements to be inspired by. We've worked on projects that have no constraints—the client will tell us "you're free to do whatever you want"—and we've found that process to be much more difficult. Lack of external constraints forces you to look inward and the work is much more insular, a reflection of yourself, and much less a collaborative process with the client, whom the work is ultimately for. In essence, it's a monologue rather than a dialogue. We believe there's a richness and value that emerges from that conversation and ultimately from those initial creative constraints.

All that being said, we do encourage our clients to push the boundaries of the original constraints. We push ourselves to think about problems holistically, even if the task at hand is very singular. It allows us to think about any given problem in new lights and means, which essentially can bring about unexpected and unique results.

You've collaborated with different creative professionals. What are some common characteristics among the most imaginative people? Or what characteristics or skills do you think professionals need to be creative thinkers and makers?
The most imaginative people I've encountered are incessantly curious by nature. They're always learning something new, almost obsessive with a subject, and always "digging deep."

Creative thinkers must also be great communicators—whether that means verbally, written or visually. They are also wonderful critics and can provide an alternate solution or at least an idea to constructively support the critique. They have the ability to be self-critical and are humble enough to know when their solution is not the best.

Lastly, some of the best creatives are amazing editors. They are constantly questioning the main goals of the project and know how to stay on task.

How do you see the role of the multifunctional designer evolving over the next decade?

In the rapidly changing landscape of design and technology, the multidisciplinary designer will become a more and more valuable asset. The notion of nonstop multitasking and efficiently navigating the onslaught of information in today's world will only propel the multidisciplinary designer forward. I can only imagine the informational world will get even more saturated, unpredictable and transformative in the future, so having the skills to navigate and make use of a varied set of expertise can only be an incredible advantage. We also think a lot in the traditional sense of the Renaissance, and how one medium can surprisingly inform another (as seen in our studio's guiding principle).

How does being able to critique your own work and take criticism from others move your work forward?

Questioning and critiquing your own work forces you to look at a problem from another perspective, to put yourself in someone else's shoes. It reveals results you may not have explored if you'd simply gone with your initial solution. It's a valuable skill in life, not just professionally, and simply encourages one to be open-minded and stay humble.

Have you ever had a project that did not go as expected? What did you learn from that experience?

We learn from each and every project, even from the buds of a project in the proposal phase, that we may not win. It forces you to look

"Nike Tech Pack Environmental Rollout
at Moynihan Station"
STUDIO: WeShouldDoItAll (WSDIA)
CLIENT: Nike
PHOTO CREDIT: Floto+Warner

"Nouvelle Vague Branding"
STUDIO: We ShouldDoItAll (WSDIA)
CLIENT: Nouvelle Vague
PHOTO CREDIT: Mastromatteo + Steen

inward: What did we do wrong? What did we do right? What questions should we have asked? Were we simply not a good fit? Truthfully projects rarely go as you expect. Sometimes you'll meet with a client and have a crystal clear idea of what the problem is and what your recommendations may be, and outside circumstances or goals shift and the end result is not what anyone could have imagined. Alternately you may be presented with a challenging problem or client and it will turn out to be a seamless process and the result will come easily. It compels you to stay fluid and keeps you on your toes; a reminder that not everything in life is as it seems and things can change in an instant.

What is your advice on working collaboratively?

Keep an open mind. Listen. Respect other ideas. Be a "Yes, and..." responder and not a "No, but..." responder—which can seriously stifle the brainstorming process and mood of the conversation! Be able to compromise and have patience; working collaboratively can be challenging, honor that. Have a sense of humor, try to keep things light and enjoyable; it makes the collaboration that much better.

JOSH OWEN

PRESIDENT, JOSH OWEN LLC (WWW.JOSHOWEN.COM)

Josh Owen is the president of his independent design atelier, Josh Owen LLC. He is also professor and chair of the Industrial Design Department at the Rochester Institute of Technology, where he teaches and develops programming for the Vignelli Center for Design Studies. His professional projects are produced by major manufacturers including Areaware, Casamania, Kikkerland, Kontextur, Loll and Umbra and have won many international awards including the I.D. Magazine Annual Design Review Award, the International Design Award, the Red Dot Design Award and six Chicago Athenaeum Good Design Awards. His work is included in the permanent design collections of the Centre Georges Pompidou in Paris, the Chicago Athenaeum, the Corning Museum of Glass, the Denver Art Museum, the Montreal Museum of Fine Arts, the Philadelphia Museum of Art, the National Museum of American Jewish History, the Rochester Institute of Technology Museum, and the Taiwan

Design Museum in Taipei. His professional and academic work has been featured in major exhibitions, numerous books on design and in such international publications as *Abitare, Domus, Dwell, Graphis, Fast Company, Forbes, Frame, Icon, Interni, Intramuros, Metropolis, Ottagono, Surface, Wired,* and *The New York Times.*

How did your study of anthropology and art affect your design practice and thinking?

Having a solid foundation in the social sciences cultivated my ability to see things in historical, cultural and critical context. It taught me to be curious about variations in approaches and to have a humanistic perspective. Studying fine arts trained me to see in ways that many do not. I learned viscerally to listen to materials and to trust my intuition. I did not realize it at the time, but in retrospect, when taken together I believe these are precisely the foundational skills needed for the role of design practitioner, one who uses design—thinking tactics to solve problems of all kinds.

You've said, "I am always looking for connections and gaps in the landscape of opportunities and things that surrounds us." How do those observations inform your creative process or work?

In academic pedagogy we often refer to "critical thinking" and even "critical making." My observational research could be referred to as "critical seeing," which is a way of studying the world—the built environment and the way in which things and people come together or remain apart. I'm an observer. Careful scrutiny creates pathways for useful contributions.

What are the most important principles for what you consider to be good design?

Dieter Rams has said it as well with his ten rules as several others have. I remember seeing a Muji poster years ago that said it something like this, "Elegance in plainness. Complexity in purity. Richness in reduction. Surprise in uniformity. Depth in minimalism.

Innovation in reuse. Sophistication in simplicity. Strategy in restraint."
I may have made up that last one.

What criteria does an industrial design have to satisfy?

It should answer a need for more than one individual, employed at a
scale relative to the need.

Considering recent developments in technology, which skills are essential for industrial designers? Why?

Aesthetic and material sensitivities, technical competence, social and
environmental awareness, analytical thinking and strategic planning.
Perhaps now, the ability to see beyond the confusion of our over-programmed, multitasked lives is more important than all. Now more
than ever, designers must have the ability to be curators of content
and to be capable of thinking beyond their bag of skills. Making good
choices is the goal.

How do you collaborate with your creative team? Why is collaboration important?

In the studio I collaborate with a revolving cast of mentees who take
the form of interns, freelancers or employees. The business partners
and stakeholders for whom I design are equally as important as the
in-house team, because without them the projects would not evolve
in the same way and would not have the same reach.

What methodology do you employ for generating new ideas, solutions or approaches? What are the tools you share with your students to generate ideas?

I always begin by trying to understand the cultures of the parties involved in the opportunity. This could be the culture that the project will be marketed in or the culture of the company or entity that
brings the problem to light. Often it means all of these. Reaching
an understanding means listening and reading, talking and seeing.
Looking at the artifacts that surround these conditions and building

Chiaroscuro Clock for Loll with XX Coatrack for Casamania
DESIGN: Josh Owen, LLC (© Josh Owen, LLC)
PHOTO CREDIT: Elizabeth Lamark

historical as well as modern and contemporary understandings is critical. I always begin with research. My students always want to propose solutions on the first day an assignment is given. I find myself telling them to slow down and think before doing.

How do you encourage your students to experiment?

Good experimentation is the byproduct of well-directed curiosity. My assignments are always strategic in their pairing of materials or subject matter with issues of some urgency to their context. Often I employ the element of competition in order to add a real-world component. This has the effect of allowing students to push the limits more. In addition, I've encouraged students to capitalize on some of the resources we have available at Rochester Institute of Technology. For example, students have access to the Vignelli Center Archives that house successful examples of innovative product development.

PJ PEREIRA

CHIEF CREATIVE OFFICER AND COFOUNDER, PEREIRA & O'DELL

PJ Pereira is chief creative officer and cofounder of Pereira & O'Dell. He has twenty years of experience in the technology and advertising industry. In just five short years, his agency has established thriving offices in San Francisco, New York and São Paulo, combining digital, traditional, design and branded content ideas for clients such as Airbnb, Intel, Toshiba, Lego, Mattel, Skype and Corona. Pereira & O'Dell has been named on both *Advertising Age* and *Creativity* A-Lists, and in 2013 was awarded an Emmy for "Outstanding New Approach" for Intel and Toshiba's social film *The Beauty Inside* as well as an unprecedented three Grand Prix at Cannes for Film, Cyber and Branded Content.

PJ has been profiled in *Creativity's* annual "Creativity 50" featuring those who have made a significant mark on the creative consciousness of our industry. PJ was also named in *Advertising Age's* "40 under 40" for his bold creative strategies.

A seasoned entrepreneur, PJ has held executive roles both at start-up agencies such as AgênciaClick, which PJ also founded, to established international agencies such as AKQA where he was executive creative director working on global accounts such as McDonalds, Nike, Coca-Cola, Visa, Red Bull, Target, and Microsoft.

He has received more than sixty international awards during the last ten years and has served as president of juries at Cannes Lions, Eurobest, London International and One Show Festivals.

What is your agency's guiding principle?

We ask ourselves: What if advertising had no history? What if advertising were invented today, the day we got the assignment? That approach frees our thinking; it frees us to use our tools to defy convention.

Look at the tools you have in hand, come up with ideas and integrate the technique instead of the media. For example, "The Beauty Inside" combines movie making with interaction. It is the second installation of social film we created for Intel and Toshiba. Sundance winner Drake Doremus directed "The Beauty Inside," the story of a guy named Alex who wakes up every day as a different person. He is always the same person on the inside but on the outside he is somebody else. When he meets Leah and falls in love everything changes for him. He knows he will see her again but she will never see him. The only way Alex can keep track of his changing identity is with the webcam on his Toshiba Portégé Ultrabook with Intel Inside.

This romance allows anyone, male or female, to play the film's lead role of Alex. Through social channels, Intel and Toshiba invited the audience to play the lead role of Alex by auditioning online. Fans could also interact with Alex on Facebook in between episodes. We created original content that leveraged social media and developed a fan base.

What kind of idea is that? A new approach to content—it's hard to categorize it. It's a different kind of idea that combines techniques for television, social media and PR to create content. It's new integration.

Emotional storytelling is at the heart of your agency's work. How do you create work that people want to engage with?

The ultimate goal is building the work to get people to want to watch it, to participate in it, to share it. If we don't see that kind of potential in an idea, we don't go with it. Essentially the story will make people want to engage with it.

We can't rely on the fact that people will watch it simply because it's there, on television or elsewhere. Today we have to work much harder to compete for people's attention with movies, games, Facebook—we have to work against anything else people spend time with; we have to make sure people will dedicate their attention to it. The bar is set much higher today.

Generating the story idea is the artistic side of the business. You consider the story you want to tell and the form to tell it in. We know the task; we know what matters. We know the strength of our brand against the competition; we know the game plan. Then you need a small group of people to start to promote it, to engage with it.

People know it's advertising, but you want them to feel something, to think, "I know this is an ad but I don't care." When you read a comment like that by a viewer, you know it's working. We want consumers to spend time with it. You don't want people to feel they've wasted their time. You want them to think, "That's pretty cool. I'm glad I spent time with it."

How do you structure a story to get people to participate?

The moment you utilize a given structure, it is too predictable. The element of surprise is what's important. Ultimately you have to find the right story—the story dictates the way it should be told. When we find the right idea, the story tells us what to do then everything else falls into place.

How do you create content that will be talked about?

We can only guess what kind of story will get results. Throw lots of ideas on the wall for consideration. When our team gets excited about an idea, we know we're on to something. The idea has to excite people—it has to be worth writing about or talking about.

What feeds your creative thinking?

Creativity is my life. The creativity is there and I use it as fuel to keep going. It is expressed through the work, through other stories. I tell stories to get people excited.

When a work is completed, I read comments and tweets about it. I watch people's reactions to the work. I learn from regular people's (not creative professionals or commentators) reactions to the last thing I've done.

What are new ways to distribute ideas?

We ask ourselves: How can we do it differently? What technology didn't we employ the last time, and would it serve this story? The story determines what we're going to do—all decisions come from there. The story always tells you the form it should take.

For example, *The Beauty Inside*—six weekly episodes hosted by Toshiba and Intel on their Facebook page—was a social story at its core. And people reacted to it in real time, unlike love stories in the past. This idea of a social film blurred the lines between branded content as a web series, traditional film and social-driven interaction.

What tactics do you employ at your agency to keep your teams fresh and always thinking creatively?

We set very high standards. Every opportunity is met optimistically.

What advice can you offer to young creatives about being a brand storyteller in the digital age?

Most of the training in school is outdated. An instructor says, "Create an integrated campaign," or "Design a mobile app." That is an old way of thinking. Students are given a problem to solve. The new generation was born as citizens of the digital world; the current pros are tourists in the digital world. I arrived as a grown-up man to the digital world—I didn't grow up in it. For the new generation—all the things that are in it are natural for them; they know how to navigate and understand the digital environment. They shouldn't let previous generations dictate to them. They should be humble but confident.

What advice can you offer to creatives?

Work harder than everyone else. Learn everything you can. There is always something to learn from every assignment. If you really pay attention and learn more, there is no way you're not going to be a superstar.

TISH SCOLNIK

CHIEF EXECUTIVE OFFICER, GRIT

Tish is the CEO and cofounder of GRIT (Global Research Innovation and Technology), a social enterprise that created the Leveraged Freedom Chair (LFC), an all-terrain wheelchair for developing countries. She graduated from Massachusetts Institute of Technology (MIT) in 2010 with a S.B. in Mechanical Engineering and a minor in applied international studies. At MIT she became hooked on using her engineering skills for public service and she put these skills to use in East Africa, Haiti and India as the LFC was developed and tested. Tish has previously worked at the World Bank and the US Department of Health and Human Services. She enjoys hiking and experimenting in the kitchen.

Please tell us about GRIT.

GRIT is a social enterprise start-up based in Boston, Massachusetts. We started as a group of engineering students at MIT, where we were working on a project to improve wheelchairs for people with

Photo credit: GRIT

disabilities in developing countries. The result was the Leveraged Freedom Chair (LFC), a lever-powered all-terrain wheelchair. After four years of testing the LFC in the field, we founded GRIT in 2012 to bring the LFC to market. We help people with disabilities get off-road and on with their lives.

How did you come up with the idea for the Leveraged Freedom Chair?
The LFC evolved through a stakeholder-driven design process, in which the end users of the product were heavily engaged. Spending time with wheelchair users in East Africa, it became apparent that existing products just didn't meet their needs. What was needed was a device that could travel long distances on rough terrain, but still be maneuverable indoors. We saw how prevalent bikes were across the developing world, and took advantage of them to make the product easy to repair, even in a village.

What role does observation play in your work?
We spent a lot of time, especially in the beginning, trying to best understand the challenges our potential users were facing. This involved spending a significant amount of time in the field, working with wheelchair users, shadowing their activities and asking questions.

How does the GRIT team collaborate?

We're a very small team and we work very closely with each other. We use regular check-ins to keep each other updated about specific projects. We also use a program called Asana to help with task management. As a small team, our partnerships with other organizations are really important. Over the course of designing the LFC we collaborated with many organizations, ranging from small and large NGOs to design firms and other academic institutions.

How did your education prepare you to generate innovative ideas?

My education at MIT gave me a lot of exposure to innovation. Through project-based classes I had the opportunity to hone my idea generation skills and see how a product evolves from an initial concept through a prototype, and in the case of the LFC, a full-blown product.

How do you bridge the gap between innovation in academia and implementation in the profession?

This is a challenge. Academia is focused on research and creating new knowledge, which doesn't always align with creating and launching an actual product. As we saw with the LFC, there was a lot of work to be done in transitioning a great prototype into a viable product. Understanding both the academic and the commercial worlds allows us to better bridge this gap.

What personal attributes and thinking skills are needed to invent or reinvent?

The ability to think outside the box, apply existing concepts in new ways, take risks, ask questions and be curious. I think curiosity and questioning are really important.

INTERVIEW WITH

BRIAN STORM

FOUNDER AND EXECUTIVE PRODUCER, MEDIASTORM

Brian Storm is founder and executive producer of the award-winning multimedia production studio MediaStorm based in Brooklyn, New York.

MediaStorm publishes diverse narratives on the human condition, offers advanced multimedia training seminars and collaborates with a diverse group of clients ranging from international corporations to individual photojournalists and artists. MediaStorm's stories and interactive applications have received numerous honors, including six Webby Awards, four Emmys, five Online Journalism Awards and the first-ever duPont Award for a Web-based production.

Prior to launching MediaStorm in 2005, Storm spent two years as vice president of News, Multimedia & Assignment Services for Corbis, a digital media agency founded and owned by Bill Gates. Storm led Corbis' global strategy for the news, sports, entertainment and historical collections and he directed the representation of world-class photographers for assignment work with a focus on creating in-depth multimedia products.

From 1995 to 2002, Storm was the first director of multimedia at MSNBC.com, a joint venture of Microsoft and NBC News, where he was responsible for the audio, photography and video elements of the site. In October of 1998, he created MSNBC's The Week in Pictures to showcase visual journalism in new media, a forerunner of the photography galleries that have become a standard offering of all major content sites today.

Storm received his master's degree in photojournalism in 1995 from the University of Missouri School of Journalism, where he ran the New Media Lab and taught Electronic Photojournalism. In 1994, he launched the first version of MediaStorm as an interactive CD-ROM production company. He serves on the Advisory Board for the Council on Foreign Relations, the W. Eugene Smith Fund, the Eddie Adams Workshop, the Alexia Foundation for World Peace, the Stan Kalish Picture Editing Workshop, Pictures of the Year, Foundation Rwanda, and Brooks Institute's Journalism School. Storm is a frequent speaker on the subject of storytelling.

Born in Minnesota, he has endured the family curse of being a lifelong fan of the Minnesota Vikings. He lives in Brooklyn, NY with his wife Elodie and their children Eva and Jasper. He can be reached via brian@mediastorm.com.

How does a story have to connect with an audience in ways it did not before?

At MediaStorm, we believe that quality storytelling is the killer app. Our mission is to convey the essence of the human experience in deeply personal, intimate and emotional ways.

We focus on stories with universal truths—those that bind us regardless of race, religion or border. Stories about common people who march through history unseen, an experience not noted in the history books. Our stories help people understand the human condition. They may not be "newsworthy" by common standards, but are essential to understanding our shared humanity. Without that, we don't understand how the world works or how it can progress.

We approach the process of storytelling with a few key things in mind:

- Everyone has a story to tell and it's not always obvious what that story is without deep reporting and an open mind.
- Time to report—along with time in postproduction—is key to a quality story.
- Quality is the central ingredient to having an impact.
- To be relevant on the web your offering needs to be either super funny or the highest quality story on the topic. That's what readers will tweet, post and share. Mediocre offerings are just noise. If you gain traction on the web, it likely means you've done something that connects to a broad swath of humanity.

Our approach to storytelling has risen out of our experience working with the limitations of other formats. Traditional media outlets, be it print, radio or TV, encourage—consciously or unconsciously—a specific type of storytelling. This can limit the depth to which a story is told, and it can limit the story's ability to be leveraged in other media.

I think the elements of great storytelling from previous formats also work online. I don't believe that we have to reinvent the elements that make a great story. Simply put, I believe a well-told tale will connect with an audience regardless of playback format.

How do you push the limits of storytelling online?

I think the innovation of our company is that we can exist at our boutique size and still have global reach. Our innovation isn't in the storytelling, it's in the business model, the tools and the distribution approach. Telling a story well is our focus more than telling it in an innovative manner.

I'm glad there are people experimenting with this issue, but it's really, really hard to build a business that is focused on storytelling at the extreme edge of technical capabilities.

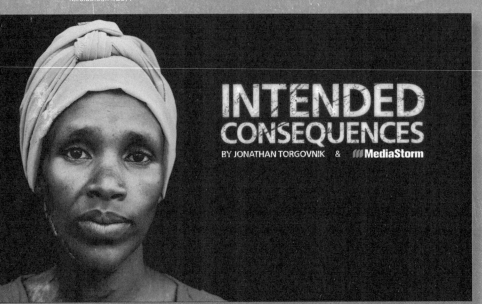

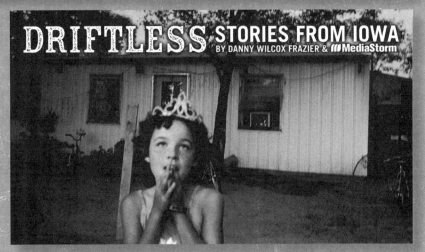

How do you leverage digital technologies to draw people in?

My first goal is for the technology to completely disappear. The last thing I want someone to think about is what camera we are using or the device that they are using to consume our story.

With that said, social media has really elevated our reach in ways that just weren't possible even ten years ago. Cortney Cleveland leads MediaStorm's social media strategy and says, "We've been able to build a community of loyal viewers and give them the tools to advocate on our behalf." This is the reason MediaStorm has never paid for advertising or promotion.

We've never been in a situation where one person could, say, watch "Intended Consequences" [about Rwanda] and then turn around and post it on Facebook for their 600 or so friends. We've never been in that situation before where people could spread things as quickly as they can now. And what are they going to spread? They're going to spread quality. It's almost like a social currency now to say, "Hey, I think this is great." That social currency just didn't exist before. Now, you see something and immediately you curate that.

How do you create work people want to share?

I don't go into a story thinking about this, but we certainly do hope that will happen. Visual storytelling thrives in the sharing economy. Social media is an increasingly visual medium. It's what people like to share, and all of the social platforms are making upgrades to accommodate this type of content (i.e., viewing films, photographs and GIFs in your feed on Twitter and Facebook).

We try to focus on stories that have a universal truth that will connect with people regardless of time or location.

A good example is "Driftless" by Danny Wilcox Frazier at http://mediastorm.com/publication/driftlessstoriesfromiowa.

It's not really a film about Iowa, it's a timeless story about land, love, craftsmanship and the economy.

Why did you produce your own video player?

We have been working on a unique toolset to run our business for the last few years that includes both a backend content management system and a front end player. Building our own technology has given us control over packaging, distribution and the business model. On the business side we have transactions in place via Pay Per Story and Subscription that allow us not only to collect money for our films, but also to have a relationship with our audience.

Because we allow anyone to embed our player we have seen ten times the playback on other websites. We have custom control over packaging and presentation of our content.

I think it's critical that you have operational excellence to enable creativity and our platform is a central element in making that happen.

Your agency creates unique content. The hardest part for many visual communicators is coming up with a viable idea for unique content. What sparks ideas for your work?

MediaStorm's approach to storytelling is built upon the great tradition of documentary still photography. I have a master's degree in photojournalism from the University of Missouri and my values were defined during the years I spent there, from 1993 to 1995.

We utilize the documentary photojournalist ethos in both the reporting and the postproduction processes. One of the main elements of this approach is to report what we see. We don't go into a story with a set idea of what the story is or should be and we don't set anything up in the reporting process. Rather, we are open to what is there.

A story that exemplifies our approach is one we did a few years ago called "The Amazing Amy" (http://mediastorm.com/training/the-amazing-amy).

We discovered Amy after seeing an award-winning picture of her taken by Melissa Golden.

I think most people see that picture and laugh. My first response was actually, She looks amazing! I thought Amy would be the type of person who was the life of the party. But MediaStorm producer Tim McLaughlin called Amy to interview her before the workshop and said to me after the call: "I think she might be the loneliest person I've ever talked to."

I was surprised to hear that and even more surprised to find out that she was only 53 years old. From looking at her picture, I thought she was much, much older. Clearly, the story we were hearing didn't match our initial perception.

During the reporting process we learned why Amy looks so old, why she performs and how lonely she really is in her life. Everyone has, at one point or another, felt extremely lonely. This is a universal human condition and it is exactly the type of focus we look for in all of our stories. If we had assumed who she was, based on our first impression of her and tried to tell a story to support that belief, we would have missed the real story of Amy's life.

When your agency offers workshops in digital storytelling, what are five points you stress?

We offer a variety of training experiences because we believe that teaching is really the best way to learn. We really love our craft and want others to build on top of our efforts.

Five points we stress include:

1. Interview techniques
2. Visual sequencing
3. Organization of assets
4. Healthy discussion/critique sessions at the appropriate times
5. Distribution strategy

What is the role of animation or motion graphics in multimedia storytelling?

MediaStorm's motion graphic artist Joe Fuller says, "Our passion for motion design stems from a desire to empower our clients with great design solutions that bring clarity to each touchpoint they have with their audiences. We start out each project with style frames and storyboards, giving clients an early understanding of the design direction and possibilities. Collaboration is key. Only with both parties on board and sharing the same vision can truly amazing work be made.

"When animating, MediaStorm draws upon the strength of its editorial expertise in constructing well-paced visuals that keep the viewer engaged. Designers carefully weave sourced imagery, graphic elements and text to well-crafted scripts and cinematic sequences."

You can see examples of how we use motion graphics here: http://mediastorm.com/clients/2013motiondesignreel.

What is the best advice you've ever given about storytelling?

My motto is to give someone a voice, don't just take their picture.

Interview © Mediastorm 2014.

STEVE VRANAKIS

EXECUTIVE CREATIVE DIRECTOR, GOOGLE CREATIVE LAB LONDON

In 1993 Steve launched one of Canada's first Internet service providers in his native Vancouver where his lifelong love for the web and technology was born. He believes that technology combined with creativity can be used as a force for good and allow for people to come up with ideas that change the world. He's worked in digital, design and advertising agencies all over the world including Vancouver, Hong Kong, San Francisco and now in London.

Some of his recent projects while at Google include: Chrome Web Lab; a series of interactive experiments connected live to the Internet from the Science Museum, London; JAM with Chrome, a web-based platform that lets you play music live with your friends from anywhere; Super Sync Sports, where you can turn your mobile phone into a game controller and sync it with your computer to play games; and Google Science Fair, a global platform that invites youth to put their ideas forward to change the world. Other notable projects include the World Wonders Project, which

135

gives access to the world's heritage sites through Street View, and the YouTube Space Lab Channel and launch video, which invited teens from all over the world to send their science experiments to space in partnership with NASA in a competition judged by Stephen Hawking. To date it has received over fifty million channel views.

Steve's work has been recognized by the Cannes Lions, Design and Art Direction (D&AD), Art Directors Club (ADC), One Show, Campaign Big Awards, British Arrows Awards, the Favourite Website Awards (FWA), the Clio Awards, Revolution, New Media Age, London International Advertising and the Andy Awards.

In December 2012, Steve was honored to speak at TEDx in Athens about making technology matter.

Please tell us about the Google Creative Lab.

A while back we tried to write a mission statement for my group based in London and we struggled. We finally got to this: A ragtag group of idealists and vagabonds. It might not be the most eloquent nor follow the conventions of company visions, but it's a great summation of who we are and what we hope to do. We're from all over the world with what we call our own special superpowers. Some of us write, film, code, design, hack, etc. When we get together we try to really push what's possible on the web and especially as it pertains to our products. We try to invent the future whilst reminding the world what they love about Google.

How do you build an enduring culture of creativity and innovation in your lab?

Two words: No fear. What we've tried to do is ensure that people who work here feel that they have the support and encouragement to try things that they may not necessarily be able to pull off immediately. They do not fear failure. Our team is given a lot of autonomy and responsibility to experiment and try different approaches to solving problems. We get to ideas very quickly by rapidly prototyping. We launch early and continue to iterate throughout the process, making things better along the way. We don't spend ages researching and validating. We do most of this in real-time.

What's your approach to storytelling in the digital age?

When we launched our recent Google Stories campaign, we wanted to ensure that we told the stories of ordinary people who used technology to achieve extraordinary things. Stuff like what Andrew Willis did by building a skate park in Hackney Wick for the local kids with nothing but reclaimed materials sourced online with Google Maps. We treat these people as heroes, the people doing the things that they believe in, and we make sure that our technology is only there to help them along the way both in their quest and in the communications we put out. Our approach to storytelling is really about telling the stories of these incredible people and their audacious ideas.

How do you create work that provokes a conversation?

People talk about things that surprise them. Unexpected things. Entertaining things. Things that people can connect to and relate to because of what they mean to everyday life. Trying to sell to people in order to get them to submit feels very antiquated. We try to inspire people. We try to show them the possibilities that the web and technology create for them—and how they can harness these tools to better themselves and the world as a whole.

How does rapid prototyping help encapsulate the big systemic idea?

In the Creative Lab we're very much driven by date, guided by instincts and informed by technology.

We look to see what people are doing or what we anticipate they will be doing. We look to phenomena in popular culture, and finally we look at all the capabilities that technology affords us and how we can use it as a force for good. Many of our products have remained in beta-testing stage for years. This allows us to keep developing them in a way that lets users know that they're not perfect yet and may not be for a little while longer. This makes for a much more transparent environment and users are generally more forgiving when things aren't spot on. We like to get to places quicker and refine things along the way.

Google Lab is known for groundbreaking solutions. Is there an approach or creative methodology or set of guiding questions your team members employ that enables this kind of work?

We follow a relatively old-school approach. It really isn't rocket science though.

1. Idea in one line. We make a poster we hang on a wall to describe the project and try to articulate the idea in a single line. No more, no less. If people don't get it as they walk by the poster, it's probably too complicated, so we start over.
2. We build a "world"—this is usually done in the form of a video. The video will begin to establish a look and feel along with a tone of voice. More importantly, we will begin to visualize what things like the user interface could look like through this video. This could go on to inform the engineers who end up building the actual product.
3. We mock stuff up. Websites, apps, whatever. We get to working models very quickly.
4. We rapidly prototype. The stuff might not look that pretty when it first comes out but the sooner we can get to proof of concept the better.
5. We make. If you follow the above you'll find yourself making 99.9 percent of the time. This is incredibly important. We try to shield our makers from as many meetings as possible to ensure that they're, well, making.

What are the habits of keen designers or creatives?

Keen designers are effectively curious creatives. They are collaborative and un-precious with their ideas. And if the ideas aren't theirs they are mature enough to still make them into something incredible. The Lab is full of sponges—people who soak stuff up. Their minds are ready to take in new theories and ideas. They look to technology, popular culture, history, the future. They keep moving. Complacency is the number one killer of creativity. Keep moving.

Have you ever had a project that did not go as expected? What did you learn from that experience?

I've worked on many, many campaigns that didn't go off as planned, failed miserably and even caught fire days before a launch. Without sounding funny, that's part of the beauty of the business we're in.

We try to make educated and informed decisions, but sometimes things don't go as planned. We believe that if you get to the answer too quickly, the problem probably wasn't hard enough to begin with. The key is to understand the *what*, the *why* and the *how*. Really learn about why something didn't deliver as expected and don't let it set you back. Come back with a vengeance. No one said that changing the world would be easy!

Some of your work involves collaboration with other experts in the Google Creative Lab as well as with other entities, such as NASA. How does collaboration enhance your work?

Collaboration is at the heart of everything we do. When we launched the Chrome Web Lab exhibition at the Science Museum we worked with about a dozen different partners. Engineers, interior architects, industrial designers, graphic designers, web developers, etc. It's incredibly important to know what you're good at, but it's even more important to know who's better than you at certain things. We've created a very unprecious environment that really promotes collaboration—everyone is credited equally. We never really call out individuals' names as very few things these days are built by one person on their own.

JESSICA WALSH

PARTNER, SAGMEISTER & WALSH (WWW.SAGMEISTERWALSH.COM)

Jessica Walsh is a designer and art director working in New York City. She is a partner at the New York-based design studio Sagmeister & Walsh. She teaches at the School of Visual Arts and speaks internationally about her work. Her work has won numerous design awards from the Type Director's Club, Art Director's Club, Society of Publication Designers (SPD), *Print* and *Graphis.* She has received various celebrated distinctions such as *Computer Arts'* "Top Rising Star in Design," Art Director's Club "Young Gun," and *Print* magazine's "New Visual Artist."

Please tell us about your personal design process.

I am interested in creating emotion- and concept-driven work with beautiful form. I always try to approach the process in a playful way with a sense of humor. I start any project by thinking and research-ing the content and the problem and figuring out how to solve that problem in the most efficient way. This might mean sketching, making mind maps or pulling reference images.

People shy away from talking about reference and inspiration images, but everyone does it. The key is to look outside your discipline for inspiration. I am inspired by all sorts of creative and noncreative fields from fashion to furniture to fine arts to psychology to astronomy. Inspiration images only become dangerous when you are pulling from within your own field and are only referencing a few projects. The more places you pull inspiration from, the more fresh and new your work will feel.

After I have an idea, I usually mock up concepts for a project in Adobe Photoshop or Illustrator. Instead of presenting many different mediocre ideas to a client, we only show one. This forces us to focus on the best solution to the project and put all of our energy and passion into that one idea. This seems less confusing to the client, and the quality of the work always ends up better.

What role does play have in your design process? How do you employ experimentation?

The heart of much of what I do is discovery through experimentation. Often the best ideas come out of spontaneous play. I think play is essentially a mind-set, where I allow myself the space and time to experiment and take risks without being afraid of failure. I know I am a very curious person with a very playful personality, so I am naturally very drawn to the conceptual and experimental phase of the creative process. But at a point when I look back on the work I've been doing, I have to realize the conceptual phase is such a tiny, tiny part of the design process. So as the years go on, I try more and more to incorporate play into the process of the execution of the work, to make it as fun and interesting and challenging as I can for myself. And of course the goal for everything I do is to communicate as well as I can with people in a way that touches people and evokes emotion.

*How did you come up with the idea of "40 Days of Dating" (http://
fortydaysofdating.com)?*

Tim Goodman and I had been friends for years, and we always made
fun of each other for having exact opposite relationship issues. Last
December, I was upset after being heartbroken by a guy I was crazy
about, and Tim was feeling confused because he was dating too many
girls at once. We were talking about our issues in line at a deli in JFK
Airport en route to Art Basel, when Tim mentioned it'd be interesting
to do a design project around the idea of dating. I instantly felt that
doing a personal project around relationships was a great idea.

People say that it takes forty days to change a bad habit. We chal-
lenged each other to think of a way we could use each other to explore
our fears and habits in relationships, and maybe even meet each other
in the middle. We started throwing crazy, nutty ideas back and forth
during the plane ride, and by the time we landed in Miami we had a
pretty elaborate and crazy plan for "40 Days of Dating."

The project was simple: Two good friends with opposite relationship issues date for forty days. We had six rules: We had to see each
other every day, go on at least three real dates a week, keep a daily
journal based on our experiences together, see a couples therapist
once a week, go on one weekend trip together, and not see, date, hook
up, or have sex with anyone else.

*What role does risk-taking play in your creative thinking? Please tell
us about your rule: Risk failure.*

The easiest thing in design is to fall back on ideas and styles you already know have worked for you or other people in the past. The work
might look great or beautiful but it's not going to feel new or fresh.
When you experiment with new ideas and risk failing on a project,
that's when the best ideas and best work comes out.

A good example of this was my project "40 Days of Dating." I had
no idea if this project would be a success or fail miserably. There was
a huge risk involved in putting so many intimate details about my

personal life online. It could have polarized friends, colleagues or clients; however, I went with my gut and we launched the project, and the positive response we received was beyond anything I could have ever imagined.

What is the role of personal projects in your creative life?

With personal projects you are allowed even more freedom to play and take risks and experiments. The things I've learned and discovered in these projects often feed back into the client work I do at the studio.

How do you bridge the gap between creativity and implementation in design?

Implementing work can be its own creative challenge that I often find interesting. We work with a team of people at the studio and often bring in outside freelancers, so I am not always the one executing the implementation.

How do you collaborate with Stefan Sagmeister and other team members at Sagmeister & Walsh?

We have three designers right now: Wade Jeffree, Santiago Carrasquilla and Zipeng Zhu. We also have two interns at any one time, who rotate every three months. Stefan or I will oversee one or two of the designers on a project. We divide up work organically based on everyone's talents, availability and passion for a given project. It's always a very collaborative process, and we are all very hands on. Depending on the project and budget we can all play a variety of roles including designer, photographer, art director, illustrator and producer.

When you teach, what do you hope your students take away from the experience?

I try to help my students find what they are most passionate about, and how design can be used as a tool to explore those interests. Many design classes teach students how to package other people's work or brands in a pretty way. Perfect kerning and font selections can be useful, but that is not what interests me most. I want to help them learn how to think conceptually about work, and how to formulate new ideas. I want to help them understand they can use design to become authors and express themselves with these tools. I want them to feel ownership over their work and be passionate about what they are doing.

RESOURCES

On Storytelling, Thinking and Writing

Ahmed, Ajaz and Stefan Olander. *Velocity: The Seven New Laws for a World Gone Digital*. (Random House, 2012).

Booker, Christopher. *The Seven Basic Plots: We Tell Stories*. (Bloomsbury, 2006).

Chaffee, John. *Thinking Critically*. 11th ed. (Cengage, 2014).

Joseph Campbell and the Power of Myth with Bill Moyers. (PBS, 1998). TV.

Campbell, Joseph. *The Hero with a Thousand Faces*. (New World Library, 2008).

Curedale, Robert. *Design Thinking*. (DCC, 2013).

Kelley, Tom and David Kelley. *Creative Confidence: Unleashing the Creative Potential Within Us All*. (Crown, 2013).

King, Stephen. *On Writing: A Memoir of the Craft*. (Scribner, 2010).

Lamott, Anne. *Bird By Bird: Some Instructions on Writing and Life*. (Anchor, 1995).

McKee, Robert. *Story: Substance, Structure, Style and the Principles of Screenwriting*. (ReganBooks, 1997).

Pinker, Steven. *Sense of Style: The Thinking Person's Guide to Writing in the 21st Century*. (Viking Adult, 2014).

Suggestions for Jumpstarting
T-Shaped Thinking

The Josef & Anni Albers Foundation. http://albersfoundation.org/teaching/josef-albers/introduction/.

Anderson, Wes. *The Grand Budapest Hotel*. (20th Century Fox, 2014). DVD.

Bucher, Stefan G. *344 Questions—The Creative Person's Do-It-Yourself Guide*. (Peachpit, 2011).

Chabon, Michael. *The Amazing Adventures of Kavalier and Clay*. (Random House, 2012).

Clark, Kenneth Sir. *Civilisation: The Complete Series*. (BBC, 2006). DVD.

Clouzot, Henri-Georges. *The Mystery of Picasso*. 1956. Film.

Cortazar, Julio. *Blow Up and Other Stories*. (Pantheon Books, 1985).

Fey, Tina. *Bossypants*. (Reagan Arthur, 2013).

Glaser, Milton. *Drawing is Thinking*. (Overlook, 2008).

Gonnella, Rose. *Design Fundamentals: Notes on Color Theory*. (Peachpit, 2014).

Gray, Peter. *Free to Learn*. (Basic Books, 2013)

Hitchcock, Alfred. *Spellbound*. (RKO, 1945). Film.

Itten, Johannes. *Design and Form: The Basic Course at the Bauhaus and Later*. (Van Nostrand Rheihold, 1975).

Ito, Mizuko. *Hanging Out, Messing Around, and Geeking Out: Kids Living and Learning with New Media*. (MIT Press, 2013).

Jenny, Peter. *Drawing Techniques*. (Princeton Architectural Press, 2013).

Kafka, Franz. *The Metamorphosis*. (Vintage, 1989.)

Kubler, George. *The Shape of Time: Remarks on the History of Things*. (Yale University, 2008).

Landa, Robin. *The Guided Sketchbook That Teaches You How to Draw*. (Peachpit, 2013).

Moore, Henry. *My Ideas, Inspiration and Life as an Artist*. (Chronicle, 1989).

Morrison, Toni. *Beloved*. (Vintage, 2004).

Ortega y Gasset, Jose. *The Dehumanization of Art and Other Essays on Art, Culture, and Literature*. (Princeton University, 1968).

Phaidon Editors. *Vitamin D2: New Perspectives in Drawing*. (Phaidon, 2013).

Roth, Phillip. *American Pastoral*. (Vintage, 1998).

Rowling, J.K. *Harry Potter and the Sorcerer's Stone*. (Scholastic, 1999).

Selznick, Brian. *The Invention of Hugo Cabret*. (Scholastic, 2007).

Richard Serra. http://www.gagosian.com/artists/richard-serra.

Tam, Amy. *The Joy Luck Club*. (Penguin, 2006).

Tharp, Twlya. *The Collaborative Habit: Life Lessons for Working Together*. (Simon & Schuster, 2013).

Tharp, Twyla. *The Creative Habit: Learn It and Use It For Life*. (Simon & Schuster, 2006).

Tyson, Neil deGrasse. *Death by Black Hole: And Other Cosmic Quandaries*. (W.W. Norton, 2014).

Wölfflin, Heinrich. *Principles of Art History: The Problem of the Development of Style in Later Art*. (Dover, 1950).

Advertising and Design Magazines and Organizations

AIGA. http://www.aiga.org.

ADC Global. http://adcglobal.org.

The American Institute of Architects: AIA Homepage. www.aia.org/.

American Society of Interior Designers (ASID). https://www.asid.org/.

Cannes Lions. http://www.canneslions.com.

Clio Awards. http://www.clioawards.com.

Communication Arts. http://www.commarts.com.

Contagious. http://www.contagious.com.

Fast Company. http://www.fastcodesign.com.

FWA - Favourite Website Awards. www.thefwa.com.

HOW Magazine. http://www.howdesign.com.

Industrial Designers Society of America - IDSA. www.idsa.org/.

Lürzer's Archive. http://www.luerzersarchive.net.

The One Club. http://www.oneclub.org.

Print Magazine. http://www.pringmag.com.

ABOUT THE AUTHOR

Robin Landa holds the title of Distinguished Professor in the Robert Busch School of Design at Kean University. She has written over twenty published books about design, creativity, advertising, branding, and drawing, including *Build Your Own Brand, Graphic Design Solutions,* 5th ed., *Advertising by Design,* 2nd ed., and *DRAW! The Guided Sketchbook That Teaches You How To Draw.* You can find translations of Robin's books in Chinese and Spanish too. Universities worldwide have adopted her books as the basis for their curricula.

Robin has won numerous awards for design, writing and teaching, including awards from the National Society of Arts and Letters, the National League of Pen Women, Creativity, New Jersey Authors Award, the Art Directors Club of New Jersey, Graphic Design USA, and Kean University Creative Research awards. She was the 2013 Kean University Professor of the Year. The Carnegie Foundation counts Robin among the "Great Teachers of Our Time." She was a finalist in the *Wall Street Journal*'s Creative Leaders competition. In 2014, Robin judged the International HOW Design Logo Competition and she is a favorite speaker at the HOW Design Conferences.

INDEX

MORE GREAT TITLES FROM HOW BOOKS

Building Better Brands

By Scott Lerman

Building Better Brands is a focused, comprehensive, and practical guide to building brands. It makes sophisticated branding development techniques accessible and actionable. This is the essential book for individuals and organizations that want to create and evolve brands.

The Strategic Designer

By David Holston

The Strategic Designer helps creatives become experts in strategy, not just design. By adopting a process that includes collaboration, context and accountability, you will learn how to think through business and design problems rationally, use your own standard process to solve problems and increase your project success rate.

Build Your Own Brand

By Robin Landa

Whether your goal is to land a new freelance job, in-house job or launch a design business, this guide is your pathway to success. *Build Your Own Brand* will help you explore, develop, distill and determine a distinctive brand essence, differentiate yourself, and create your visual identity and personal branding statement.

**Find these books and many others at
MyDesignShop.com or your local bookstore.**